GLOBETR

CW00326947

Travel

MILAN
AND THE ITALIAN LAKES

ROWLAND MEAD

NEW
HOLLAND

★★★ Highly recommended
★★ Recommended
★ See if you can

First edition published in 2003
by New Holland Publishers (UK) Ltd
London • Cape Town • Sydney • Auckland
10 9 8 7 6 5 4 3 2 1
website: www.newhollandpublishers.com

Garfield House, 86 Edgware Road
London W2 2EA, United Kingdom

80 McKenzie Street
Cape Town 8001, South Africa

14 Aquatic Drive, Frenchs Forest,
NSW 2086, Australia

218 Lake Road, Northcote,
Auckland, New Zealand

Distributed in the USA by
The Globe Pequot Press, Connecticut

Copyright © 2003 in text: Rowland Mead
Copyright © 2003 in maps:
Globetrotter Travel Maps
Copyright © 2003 in photographs:
Individual photographers as credited (right)
Copyright © 2003 New Holland Publishers (UK) Ltd

All rights reserved. No part of this publication
may be reproduced, stored in a retrieval system
or transmitted, in any form or by any means,
electronic, mechanical, photocopying, recording
or otherwise, without the prior written permission
of the publishers and copyright holders.

ISBN 1 84330 468 6

Although every effort has been made to ensure that
this guide is up to date and current at time of going
to print, the Publisher accepts no responsibility or
liability for any loss, injury or inconvenience
incurred by readers or travellers using this guide.

Keep us Current
Information in travel guides is apt to change, which
is why we regularly update our guides. We'd be
grateful to receive feedback if you've noted something we should include in our updates. If you have
new information, please share it with us by writing
to the Publishing Manager, Globetrotter, at the
office nearest to you (addresses on this page). The
most significant contribution to each new edition
will receive a free copy of the updated guide.

Publishing Manager (UK): Simon Pooley
Publishing Manager (SA): Thea Grobbelaar
DTP Cartographic Manager: Genené Hart
Editor: Melany McCallum
Cartographer: Nicole Engeler
Design and DTP: Lellyn Creamer
Picture Researcher: Colleen Abrahams
Consultant: Tracey Gambarotta
Proofreader: Thea Grobbelaar

Reproduction by Hirt & Carter (Pty) Ltd, Cape Town
Printed and bound in Hong Kong by Sing Cheong
Printing Co. Ltd.

Photographic Credits:
Axiom/Renzo Frontoni: pages 37, 38, 42; **Caroline
Jones:** pages 9, 26, 113, 118, 119; **Rowland Mead:**
pages 11, 27, 31, 45, 46, 47, 50, 56, 58, 59, 61, 62, 63,
73, 78, 80, 81, 82, 83, 89, 99, 108; **PhotoBank/
Jeanetta Baker:** pages 93, 94, 96; **PhotoBank/
Peter Baker:** pages 66, 68, 71, 72, 92, 95, 104;
PhotoBank/Gary Goodwin: pages 17, 102, 107, 112;
Robin Smith: pages 10, 86, 91; **J. Snyders:** pages 4,
12, 13, 14, 16, 18, 19, 21, 22, 23, 24, 25, 28, 33, 40, 41,
53, 54, 55, 76, 77; **Sylvia Cordaiy Photo Library/
Geoffrey Taunton:** title page, page 44; **Sylvia
Cordaiy Photo Library/Johnathan Smith:** pages 6,
70, 106, 110, 111; **Travel Ink/Ronald Badkin:** pages
7, 105; **Travel Ink/Andrew Cowin:** cover page, page
8; **Travel Ink/David Forman:** pages 34, 74, 75;
Travel Ink/Alex Hinds: pages 36, 114; **Travel
Ink/Martin Wilson:** pages 116, 117.

Cover: *View across Lake Como, near Menaggio.*
Title Page: *Milan Cathedral.*

CONTENTS

1
Introducing Milan and the Italian Lakes

Many people consider that wealthy Milan should really be the capital of Italy. Admittedly, it does not have the ancient remains of Rome, the waterborne charms of Venice or the elegance of Florence, but Milan is the industrial and commercial powerhouse of the country. It differs from the somnolent south of Italy – no long afternoon siestas for the Milanese, who like to think of themselves as being more northern European in attitude. They pride themselves on their timekeeping, their industry and their ability to make things function properly. Milan's population of 1.4 million accounts for barely four per cent of the Italian people and yet they contribute around a quarter of the country's tax returns!

This application and creativity is probably explained by Milan's geographical position. Located on the fertile Lombardy Plain drained by the River Po, Milan's backdrop is the snowcapped Alps. Throughout its history, invaders from the north, from the Lombards to the Habsburgs, have poured through the Alpine passes bent on conquest, but often staying to settle and thereby adding their skills to the population's accomplishments.

Although Milan can boast few of the ancient monuments that grace Rome, there is enough of historical interest to satisfy a tourist for many days. Few could fail to be impressed by the imposing Gothic Duomo, or cathedral, which took over 500 years to complete and which is resplendent with 135 carved pinnacles. No visitor would want to leave Milan without seeing Leonardo's *Last Supper* in the refectory of Santa Maria

Top Attractions

*** The Duomo:** Milan's cathedral, the finest Gothic cathedral in Italy.
*** The Arena at Verona:** the Roman amphitheatre that seats 25,000 people for summer operas.
*** Borromean Islands:** three beautiful islands on Lake Maggiore.
** Villa Carlotta:** on Lake Como – the most opulent of all the lakeside villas.
** La Scala:** Milan's world-famous opera house.
** Leonardo's *Last Supper:*** fresco at the church of Santa Maria delle Grazie.

Opposite: *Some of the many statues on the façade of Milan's cathedral.*

Above: *Limone on Lake Garda, which can easily be reached from Milan.*

delle Grazie or enjoying an opera at La Scala. There is much more. There are galleries and museums by the score. Who could resist shopping in the Via Monte Napoleone? Here the Milanese passion for style and fashion comes to the fore and the visitor can browse in the boutiques at the creations of Gucci, Versace and Armani. Football fans, too, are catered for and they can watch a match at the San Siro Stadium (*see* page 47).

Furthermore, it is easy to leave the city of Milan behind and within an hour be in the **Italian Lakes** region. Lakes such as Como, Maggiore and Garda are long and narrow in shape and owe their origins to the Ice Age, when glaciers moved down from the Alps eroding deep valleys that later filled with meltwater. Throughout history the lakes have been the haunt of the wealthy, from the Roman Pliny to the pop stars of today. The shores are graced by elegant villas and tree-lined promenades backed by terraces of citrus fruit and olives, with the snowcapped Alps forming a stunning back-drop. The Milanese flock here for their relaxation, mixing with tourists from many parts of the world, many of whom come back time and again.

THE LAND
Mountains and Rivers

The scenery around Milan and the northern Italian Lakes owes much of its present-day appearance to the **Ice Age**, which took place in the Quaternary geological period. The Alps, a mountain range that has its origins in the action of volcanoes and the movement of the earth's plates, was one of the first parts of Europe to be affected when the Ice Age started around a million years ago. Glaciers flowed slowly down from the Alps along pre-existing river-worn valleys towards the plains to the south. The glaciers scoured out

---

FACT FILE ON MILAN

Size: covers an area of 182km² (70 sq miles).
Position: 122m (400ft) above sea level in the Po Basin.
Population: 1.4 million. The second largest city in Italy and the 10th largest in Europe. Greater Milan has a population of 3.78 million.
Population density: 1900 per km².
Education: Milan has three universities, the country's most prestigious business school, a polytechnic, and academies of music and art.

the valleys to a considerable depth, often below sea level, while at the snouts of the glaciers, streams washed out fine rock material known as moraine. Between 10,000 and 20,000 years ago the climate became milder and the glaciers retreated. Streams filled the scoured out valleys forming the **ribbon lakes** so typical of northern Italy. The southern outlets of the lakes were often dammed by the moraine, deepening the lakes even further. The deepest point of Lake Como, for example, is 410m (1345ft), with the lake's bed 300m (984ft) below sea level. Other types of moraine along the lake shores provide favoured spots for settlement or agriculture. Today the snow and ice have retreated back to the highest parts of the Alps, remaining throughout the summer to form a magnificent photogenic backdrop for the lakes area. The hilly area around the southern parts of the lakes is often termed the **Pre-Alps**.

Further south, the glacial material has been reworked by the **River Po** and its tributaries, such as the Sésia, the Ticino, the Adda and the Adige, to form a fertile plain. In the past the rivers flooded regularly, leaving a layer of silt that further added to the plain's fertility. Today, the Po Valley is the richest agricultural region in Italy, growing rice, grapes, maize and a variety of fruit and vegetables. The Po, which is Italy's longest river, has also been important for navigation, and large ships can still reach as far inland as Pavia, just 38km (24 miles) to the south of Milan. The river was a safe transport route to bring stone for the construction of churches and palaces, transport soldiers in times of war, and carry goods from all over the world into the heart of northern Italy.

To the south of the Po Valley are the **Apennine Hills**, which form the spine of Italy. On a clear day it is possible to stand on the Apennines and see the snowcapped wall of the Alps rising above the haze of the Po Valley.

> **ITALY'S LAKES**
>
> It is estimated that there are around 1500 lakes in Italy. They have been formed in a variety of ways. The most common are the **alpine glacial lakes**, which are small, usually round and occupy cirques where glaciers were originally formed. **Crater lakes** are found in the craters of extinct volcanoes, mainly in the south of Italy. **Coastal lakes** are in the form of lagoons and can be seen along the Adriatic coast. The largest and most scenically spectacular lakes are the **ribbon lakes**, such as Lake Como in northern Italy, which occupy the over-deepened valleys carved out by glaciers in the Ice Age.

Below: *Bellagio, one of many popular resorts on Lake Como.*

THE RIVER PO

With a length of 405km
(251 miles), the River Po is
Italy's longest river. It rises in
the Cottian Alps and enters
the Adriatic Sea, 56km
(35 miles) south of Venice.
It is navigable as far as Pavia,
38 km (24 miles) south of
Venice. Its main tributaries
are the Ticino, the Adda and
the Adige. The River Po plain
is the richest agricultural
area in Italy. It is also Italy's
most polluted river –
136,000 tonnes of nitrates,
250 tonnes of arsenic and
60 tonnes of mercury are
pumped into the river daily.

Below: *Although the
lakes have mild winters,
the snowcapped Alps to the
north provide a photogenic
backdrop.*

Climate

The Po Valley and the Italian lakes have unusual
weather in that the area lies at the junction of the
Mediterranean and Alpine climatic types and has the
best (and worst!) features of both. The city of **Milan** has
cold, raw winters, with a January average of 2ºC (36ºF).
Snow is experienced regularly and fog can last for days
on end, both in the city and on the surrounding plains.
The summer months of July, August and September can
be unbearably hot and sticky, with July averaging 26ºC
(78ºF). August can be particularly humid and everyone
who can do so leaves Milan for more agreeable climatic
venues. Rain falls throughout the year, falling in late
summer in thunderstorms.

The **Italian lakes** have a more moderate climate. The
Alps shield the lakes from the more extreme weather in
winter, when temperatures range from 4ºC (39ºF) to 6ºC
(43ºF), allowing a wide range of plants to survive. Snow
is usually confined to the higher ridges between the
lakes. Summers are hot, with July temperatures averaging 24ºC (75ºF) at Lake Como and 25ºC (77ºF) at Lake
Garda. Rain falls throughout the year, but mainly as
spectacular thunderstorms in late summer. These can
reverberate around the Alps for days. The heat of the
summer is tempered by refreshing breezes blowing
down the lakes. These winds can reverse their direction
according to the time of
day, providing good
conditions for sailors
and windsurfers.

Climatically, the best
time to visit the lakes is
either in spring, when the
flowers, blossom and bird-
song are at their best, or
autumn, especially late
September, when the
temperatures are balmy
and the autumn colours
are spectacular.

Wildlife

It has to be said that northern Italy is not one of Europe's prime wildlife sites. This is largely owing to the hunting and shooting that has been traditional in the country for centuries.

Don't expect to see much wildlife in **Milan**, apart from the thousands of pigeons that inhabit its squares and a few bedraggled specimens of wildfowl on the lakes in the city's parks. The situation is little better on the **Lombardy Plain**, where during the hunting season from August to March, and particularly on Sundays, the fields reverberate with the thunder of guns as hunters with their feathered Alpine hats blast at everything that moves, whether the creature is protected or not.

Around the **lakes**, the situation improves. Water birds such as mute swans, mallards and coots can be seen everywhere along the lake shores. There are encouraging numbers of great crested grebes and, where there is more shelter and vegetation, little grebes often breed. There is also the chance of seeing a kingfisher on boughs hanging over the water. Fish abound, particularly trout, charr and pikeperch (which northern Europeans will know as zander). There is an active fishing industry, especially on Lake Maggiore, and these fish all appear on restaurant menus. The forested slopes of the lakes are home to many species of woodpecker, including the large black woodpecker, plus, in the summer, many species of warbler, redstarts and flycatchers.

At the northern end of the lakes, on the approach to the **Alps**, the amount of wildlife increases. The coniferous forests are the habitat of a variety of mammals including red squirrels, wild boar, and introduced deer. Badgers and wildcats are also around but as they are nocturnal they are unlikely to be seen. Predators include stoats and foxes.

Above: *Mute swans are found on all of the northern Italian lakes.*

THE MARMOT

Anyone visiting the Alps to the north of the Italian lakes in summer stands a good chance of seeing a marmot (*Marmota montis* – literally mountain mouse). It lives in the Alps above 1800m (6000ft) and spends much of the daylight hours feeding on vegetation. It lives in burrows and hibernates during the winter. It is most vulnerable to predators in spring when it emerges from hibernation and its senses are not fully alert. Its warning call is an eerie, high-pitched shriek.

COMPARATIVE CLIMATE CHART	MILAN				MAGGIORE				GARDA			
	WIN	SPR	SUM	AUT	WIN	SPR	SUM	AUT	WIN	SPR	SUM	AUT
	JAN	APR	JULY	OCT	JAN	APR	JULY	OCT	JAN	APR	JULY	OCT
AVERAGE TEMP. °C	1	10	22	12	5.2	12.9	23.9	10.1	4	13.2	24.5	14.7
AVERAGE TEMP. °F	35	51	72	54	41	54	74	50	39	55	76	58
RAINFALL mm	62	82	47	75	90	61	20	22	31	62	72	89
RAINFALL in	3	3	2	3	4	3	1	1	1	3	3	4

Above: *Carpets of wild flowers can be seen in spring in the Alpine meadows to the north of the lakes.*

Above the tree line, chamois and ibex can be seen in good numbers. In many areas marmots, a mouse-like creature the size of a cat, are so widespread that lynx have been introduced to control their numbers. Their main predator, however, is the huge golden eagle, which also takes mountain hares. Other raptors include the short-toed eagle (which can hover like a kestrel), the honey buzzard and the long-eared owl. The rocky peaks are the natural habitat of the alpine chough, which is immediately recognizable by its electric call.

Italy has some 15 species of snake, some of which are venomous. A few of these can be found in northern Italy, but the chance of a visitor encountering one is slight. Lizards, however, are common and include the green lizard, the wall lizard, the gecko and the huge ocellated lizard. Butterflies are prolific in the summer, when the visitor can expect to see the small Apollo, clouded yellow, grayling, ringlet and a host of small blues.

However, it is the **flora** that draws many visitors to northern Italy, particularly in spring and early summer. The mild winter climate of the lakes (Garda has only frozen over once and that was in 1701) means that a wide range of exotic flowers, shrubs and trees can be grown in the gardens and hotel grounds along the waterside. The gardens on Isola Madre and Isola Bella on the Borromean Islands of Lake Maggiore are a wonderful example. Try not to miss the azaleas and rhododendrons at Villa Carlotta on Lake Como during April and May.

Many visitors are attracted to the Alps where wild flowers such as the gentian, edelweiss and saxifrage appear in spring after the snows have melted. Lower down the slopes, orchids like the lady's slipper are now fully protected. Other plants such as arnica are collected for their medicinal properties.

THE GOLDEN EAGLE

Visitors to the northern parts of the Italian lakes might be lucky enough to get a glimpse of the golden eagle (*Aquia chrysaetos*). With a wingspan of 2m (6ft), it can be seen soaring over the alpine meadows and forests in search of prey such as mountain hares, ptarmigan and marmots.

Wildlife Protection in Northern Italy

Italy is often the despair of its neighbours in northern Europe when it comes to environmental matters. In theory and on paper, there is a whole series of conservation bodies ranging from National Parks (*Parchi Nazionali*) down to small Nature Oases (*Oasi Naturali*). In practice, conservation and protection are slipshod and the responsibility of a confusing variety of bodies. Officially some three per cent of the country is protected – compare this with 21 per cent for the United Kingdom and 28 per cent for third-world Costa Rica. The main problems are bureaucracy and the vested interests of bodies such as the hunting lobby, which prevent the organizations from carrying out their environmental responsibilities. The liming and netting of birds is still common, while hunting and poaching of protected species continues to take place. The nearest protected areas to the Italian lakes are the **Adamello-Brenta** to the northwest of Lake Garda and the **Val Grande** and the **Alta Valsesia** reserves, which lie between Lake Maggiore and the peaks of Monte Rosa.

> ### THE GREAT CRESTED GREBE
>
> One of the most common birds on the Italian lakes is the great crested grebe. The breeding adult is easily identified by its black ear tufts and black frills on the face. Its courtship display, when it rears out of the water and the male presents weeds to the female, is one of the magic moments of bird-watching. Great crested grebes build floating nests of aquatic vegetation. After hatching, the baby grebes often hitch a lift on the adults' backs.

HISTORY IN BRIEF

The history of the Lombardy Plain and the city of Milan in particular has been a gruesome catalogue of invasions, sieges, plagues, wars and, in recent years, bombings. It is a characteristic of the area that it has always pulled itself together, recovered and returned to prosperity.

Below: *There is little in the way of wildlife in the city, but there are plenty of pigeons for tourists to feed.*

Early Days

The retreating ice sheets left behind a fertile landscape which was quickly occupied as early as Bronze-Age times by Ligurians from the west and Etruscans from the south. Milan itself was probably founded around 600BC by the Insubres, who were a Celtic tribe from

THE ICE AGE

The Ice Age began around one million years ago and ended between 10,000 and 20,000 years ago, depending on latitude and height above sea level. The higher peaks of the Italian Alps still have a permanent cover of snow and ice. Glaciers flow down from these areas, but they have been retreating in recent years due to global warming. Ice was responsible for much of the scenery of northern Italy.

Gaul. In 222BC, the Romans arrived in the area, and Milan became the major settlement of Cisalpine Gaul, quickly becoming the Empire's second largest city after Rome. In the 3rd century the Roman Empire was divided into two by Diocletian, and Rome became the capital of the Western Empire. In 313, Constantine issued the Edict of Milan, which officially recognized Christianity as a religion. Thereafter the city became an important religious centre, helped by the appointment of the respected Sant'Ambrogio (Ambrose) as Bishop of Milan.

The fall of the Roman Empire marked a period of decline for Milan, which could not defend itself against barbarians such as the Huns and the Goths who both pillaged the city. The next group to invade were the Lombards, who set up their court at Pavia and gave their name to the province that covers most of the area described in this book. The *longobardi* (see panel, page 14) were not entirely vandals, however, and they set up law courts and eventually converted to Christianity. They were defeated by the Franks led by Charlemagne in AD774, and Milan regained its position as the main town of the area.

The Middle Ages

Below: *The old part of Bergamo has a wealth of city walls, gates, towers and historic churches.*

The economy revived under the Franks and, helped by a series of influential bishops, Milan, in 1045, declared itself a *comune* or city-state. The next three centuries were characterized by conflict between Milan and other city-states such as Pavia, Cremona and Como. A new city wall was

built, but this was demolished in 1162 by Frederick Barbarossa on behalf of Como. The walls were speedily reconstructed and the Lombard League was set up under the leadership of Milan to afford additional protection. These inter-city struggles were typified by support for either the pro-pope *Guelfs* or the *Ghibellines* who represented the emperor.

The Dynastic Families

The 13th century saw the first of the dynastic families come to power. This was the Torriani family, who were part of the pro-pope faction. They were not to last long, however, as they were soundly defeated in 1277 by the **Viscontis** representing the Ghibelline element. By this time Milan had a population of around 200,000 – making it probably the largest city in Europe. The greatest of the Viscontis was Gian Galeazzo (1351–1402) who bought the title of Duke of Milan and at the height of his power controlled most of northern Italy. He also commissioned the building of the Duomo, the Castello and many palaces. Unfortunately, Gian Galeazzo died from the plague in 1402 and within 40 years the dynasty had died out.

Milan immediately declared itself the Ambrosian Republic, but within three years the city had come under the control of the first of the **Sforza** family. Francesco Sforza, who claimed the dukedom because he had married an illegitimate daughter of the Viscontis, adopted a different approach from the preceding dynasty, preferring to acquire peace for the city rather than expansion. The castle was rebuilt and renamed the Castello Sforzesco, and work was started on the Ospedale Maggiore. The golden age of the Sforzas came with Francesco's son Ludovico el Moro, who was a great patron of the arts. He brought to his court such talents as Leonardo da Vinci (1452–1519) and the architect Donato Bramante (1444–1514) who restored many of Milan's churches.

Ludovico's downfall came when, in 1494, he encouraged Charles VIII of France to invade Naples. Alarmed by their success, he led a coalition of forces to drive the French out of Italy. After some initial success, he was forced out of power in 1499 by Louis XII, who marched into Milan and claimed the city for himself. The population, who were weary of paying taxes to support the Sforza regime, welcomed Louis with open arms, while Ludovico was obliged to spend the rest of his life in exile.

Above: *The tower of this church near Lake Como is typical of many in the area, which have a top-heavy appearance.*

MASTER BUILDERS OF COMO

The magnificent churches and cathedrals of northern Italy owe much to the *Maestri Comocini* – the master builders from the Como area. They were travelling groups of architects and stonemasons who used the marble and granite of their home area to wonderful effect. They worked from the 7th to the 17th century and were probably at their peak during the 12th century. Their work can be seen, not only in northern Italy, but as far afield as Poland and Russia.

Above: *Finding a postbox to send cards and letters home is not difficult in the cities of northern Italy.*

SINISTER LOMBARDS

One of the first tribes to take advantage of the fall of the Roman Empire were the Lombards who flooded into northern Italy in 568. It has often been suggested that this Germanic group got its name from their long beards, but in fact it was from their long *bardi*, or poleaxes, that terrified their enemies. They had a reputation for barbarism supported by the story of their king, named Alboin, who forced his wife Rosmunda to drink from her father's skull. In revenge for this indignity she stabbed him to death. The Lombards conquered much of Italy and in fact came nearer to unifying the country than any group for the next 14 centuries. The Lombards' name also lingers on, with a street in London, a region of Italy, a river plain, and even a political party.

Foreign Domination

For the next three centuries Milan and the Plain of Lombardy were to languish under foreign powers. Virtually the only good to come out of this period was the spell in office of the Archbishop of Milan, San Carlo Borromeo (1538–84). He was a patron of the arts, built numerous churches and social institutions for the poor, and got rid of the corruption that was rife in the area. The plague of 1630 brought Milan's population down to around 60,000 and this was a low point in the city's social and economic standing.

The French were soon removed by the Spanish, who had control over Milan until the War of the Spanish Succession (1701–13), after which the Austrians took over. Enlightened despots such as Maria Theresa (1740–80) and her son Joseph II did much to introduce economic reforms during this period. The Austrians, in turn, were forced out by the French, and when Napoleon's army entered Milan, the troops were welcomed as liberators. Napoleon proclaimed the Cisalpine Republic and in 1800 he crowned himself King of Italy in Milan Cathedral. Napoleon modernized the city, reforming the administration, setting up schools on the *lycée* model, and starting many public building projects. The population, however, were heavily taxed and many of Milan's art treasures were removed to France. The Milanese were therefore not too unhappy when the Napoleonic Empire collapsed and the Austrian forces returned in 1814. Austrian control was officially recognized at the Congress of Vienna in 1815, and the Habsburgs were to remain in charge of the city for the next 50 years.

Unification

Movements for uniting the country immediately began to appear. The most influential figures were Guiseppi Mazzini (1805–72), an important political agitator; Guiseppi Garibaldi (1807–82), a charismatic military

HISTORICAL CALENDAR

600BC The Etrucscans settle in Lombardy Plain.

222BC Roman Conquest. Mediolanum (Milan) becomes the capital of the Western Roman Empire.

AD313 Constantine the Great issues the Edict of Milan allowing tolerance of the Christian faith.

374 Ambrose (Sant'Ambrogio) becomes Bishop of Milan.

476 Fall of the Western Roman Empire.

568 Lombards invade northern Italy, making Pavia their capital.

773 Charlemagne conquers the Lombards, incorporating their land into the Frankish Empire.

1045 Milan becomes an autonomous *comune*.

1162 Milan is taken by Frederick Barbarossa.

1176 The Lombard League defeats Barbarossa at Legnano.

1277 The Visconti dynasty begin their rule over Milan.

1477 Francesco Sforza is made Duke of Milan. Later Ludovico el Moro patronizes Leonardo da Vinci as well as other artists and architects.

1499 Milan occupied by the French under Louis XII.

1525 Milan becomes part of the Habsburg empire.

1540–1706 Spanish rule.

1701–13 War of the Spanish Succession. At its conclusion the Duchy of Milan comes under Austrian rule.

1796–1814 Napoleon conquers Lombardy and makes Milan the capital of his Cisalpine Republic.

1815 Milan once again becomes Austrian.

1815–59 The rise of the *Risorgimento* independence movement. Milan becomes the industrial and financial capital of a free Italy.

1919 After World War I Mussolini founds the Fascist movement in Milan.

1939–45 Milan suffers serious bombing during Allied raids. Mussolini is shot while fleeing to Switzerland in 1945.

1950s Milan leads Italy's postwar economic revival.

1960s and 70s Student unrest and terrorism.

1992 The *Tangentopoli* corruption scandals focus on Milan.

1995 Maurizio Gucci, the fashion designer, is murdered in Milan.

1997 Gianni Versace is murdered in Florida.

2002 Euro currency is introduced.

figure; and Count Camillo Cavour (1810–61), who owned the newspaper *Il Risorgimento*, which gave its name to the unification movement. The first action came in March 1848 when the Milanese staged a revolt known as *Cinque Giornate* – the five days that the revolt lasted. The insurrection was brutally crushed by the Austrians, but the unification movement was gathering pace. Supported by Louis Napoleon, the Austrians were defeated at Magenta in 1859 and the northern part of Italy was united under Piedmont. Victor Emmanuel II of Piedmont marched into Milan through the triumphal arch that was built by Napoleon and which is now known as the Arch of Peace.

Unification was only half complete, but Garibaldi's forces soon overthrew the Bourbons in the south of the country and King Victor Emmanuel II was proclaimed King of Italy in February 1861. Complete unity was achieved with the addition of Venice in 1866 and Rome in 1871.

NAPOLEON – SAINT OR SINNER?

When Napoleon marched into Milan, the city welcomed him with open arms. Eighteen years later, with the collapse of the Napoleonic Empire, the Milanese had had enough and were glad to see the back of him. On the credit side, he had established Milan as the capital of the Cisalpine Republic, inaugurated extensive public works, reformed the education and legal systems on French lines, founded Milan's Fine Arts Academy and the Brera Museum and Gallery. On the other hand, his administration imposed high taxes on the populace and plundered art treasures from churches and private collections. Perhaps Napoleon's most lasting memorial is that he put into many people's minds the potential for a single unified Italian state.

For the remainder of the 19th century Milan concentrated on building up its economic base. The industrial revolution generated a variety of industries, including chemicals and textiles, while in the city centre the stock exchange and banks flourished and the opera house established its reputation. Milan was now the business and commercial capital of the newly united country.

World War I and the Growth of Fascism

After being neutral at the start of the war, Italy entered the conflict on the Allied side in 1915, expecting some rewards in the form of land at the conclusion. The war turned out to be a disaster for Italy. Its army was ill-equipped and at one battle alone – Caporetto in 1917 – half a million Italians died. It was estimated that of the 5.5 million Italians who were mobilized some 40 per cent were killed or wounded.

It was not surprising that after the war there was considerable social and economic unrest in Italy and the **Fascist** movement came to the fore. Both the Fascist movement and its leader, Benito Mussolini, had close links with Milan. Mussolini became dictator of Italy in 1922 and his plans for buying weapons of war made him popular with the middle-class industrialists of Milan.

World War II

Mussolini took Italy into the war, making a pact with Hitler. The Allies invaded Italy in 1943 and later that year the Italian government signed an armistice with the Allies. The Germans now took control of the north of the country and established a puppet government at the resort of Salò on Lake Garda. It was during 1943 that Milan, with its heavy industry, became a target for Allied bombers, which inflicted heavy damage on the city. Meanwhile the Italians had formed a determined Resistance movement that continually

Below: *Even the most discerning shopper will find plenty of interest in central Milan.*

harassed the Germans. It was these partisans who finally caught Mussolini as he was trying to escape to Switzerland. He was shot along with his mistress, and his body was later strung up from the roof of a petrol station in Milan's Piazza Loreto, where some partisans had been shot a few weeks earlier.

Above: *This Roman amphitheatre is the venue for outdoor opera performances during July and August.*

The Postwar Years

In 1946 King Victor Emmanuel III abdicated and Italy voted in a referendum to abolish the monarchy. The postwar period was typified by political instability. Most governments were coalitions and they fell and were replaced with regularity – there were nearly 60 governments between the end of World War II and the close of the century. Milan, however, led the postwar 'economic miracle'. Helped by generous Marshall Aid, the city re-established its heavy industry. Later came new high-tech industries, while the banks and the stock market thrived. Less savoury were the student protests of the 1960s and the terrorist activity of the 1970s.

Even more sensational were the bribery and corruption scandals of the early 1990s, when Judge Antonio de Pietro lifted the lid on the racketeering and bribery that was rife in politics and business. Milan became known as *Tangentopoli* or 'Bribe City'. Milan also produced **Silvio Berlusconi**, a self-made man who became a media mogul and eventually, in 2001, the country's prime minister.

Art and Architecture

The earliest architecture to survive dates from **Roman** times. Examples are few, however, and confined to a handful of villas on the southern shores of Lake Garda, the forum at Brescia, and the magnificent amphitheatre at Verona. In Milan, there are some remains of the curving walls of the circus, which must have been one of the largest constructions in the Roman Empire, while a few private houses in the same area have some fragmented

---

CAVOUR (1810–61)

Count Camillo Benso di Cavour was the brains behind the unification of Italy. He was born in Turin, but for many years he worked for the Kings of Sardinia who became its first king. It was to his great personal satisfaction that when Italy became united it was Victor Emmanuel II of Sardinia who became first king. An able politician, Cavour believed that progress lay not in revolution but in social and economic progress. Sadly, he died a year after Italy achieved unification.

Above: *Como's cathedral is a curious mixture of Gothic and Renaissance architecture.*

mosaics. By far the most interesting Roman architecture in the city lies outside the Church of San Lorenzo, where a row of 16 Corinthian columns dating from the 2nd or 3rd century AD have been erected, having been brought there from some unidentified temple.

The **Romanesque** period was one of the most vital phases in Italian art and architecture, Lombardy standing out for its numerous churches of quality. The Lombard Romanesque had a style of its own, reflecting the architecture of southern Germany, with essential simplicity alongside round arches, and decoration confined to the apse or main portal. The work was carried out by travelling bands of master builders such as the *Maestri Comacini* from Como. Classic examples from this period include Sant'Ambrogio in Milan, San Fedele in Como, and the Basilica of Santa Maria Maggiore in Bergamo.

So successful was the Lombard form of Romanesque that the **Gothic**, so popular in France, was resisted in northern Italy. The glorious exception is the Duomo in Milan, which is probably the most strongly Gothic religious building in Italy. The Lombard builders never totally adapted the Gothic style, rejecting the striving for height and the resulting flying buttresses, but maintaining the thick walls and horizontal lines. At this time, a small number of artists and sculptors were beginning to throw off the shackles of Byzantine art, particularly in sculpture and in early frescoes.

The **Renaissance** marked a rebirth of art and science as the Greek and Roman ideals were 'rediscovered'. The movement originated in Florence and quickly spread to other parts of Italy, including Lombardy, where the wealth of the region was poured into the sponsorship of talent by merchants and bankers. Ludovico il Moro brought Leonardo da Vinci into his court, and his many talents were to inspire a whole range of followers, such

> ### DONATO BRAMANTE – MASTER ARCHITECT
>
> Donato Bramante (1444–1514) has always been recognized as the greatest Renaissance architect in Italy. Born in Urbino, he was brought to Milan by Ludovico el Moro. He worked on a number of churches in the city, including San Satiro, the tribune of Santa Maria delle Grazie and the cloisters of Sant'Ambrogio, and drew up a new plan for the cathedral at Pavia. While in Milan, Bramante also painted and wrote poetry, and it is believed that he had close relations with Leonardo da Vinci. Bramante left, in 1499, for Rome, where he continued his glittering career working, among other projects, on the rebuilding of St Peter's.

as the painter Bernardino Luini (d. 1532) and the sculptor Cristoforo Solari (1439–1525). There are some superb examples of Renaissance architecture in Milan, first appearing in the middle of the 15th century, when Francesco Sforza brought in Filarete to design the Ospedale Maggiore (based on an example in Florence). Later Ludovico il Moro hired the incomparable Donato Bramante (1444–1514), who contributed the apse of San Satiro, the cloisters of Sant'Ambrogio and the wonderful tribune of Santa Maria delle Grazie. Elsewhere in the region, Brescia became a major centre for Renaissance painting. Mantua, with the wealthy Gonzaga family spending freely, sponsored much Renaissance work. The court painter here was Andrea Mantegna (d. 1506), who established a considerable reputation for his frescoes. The Palazzo Tè, just outside the city, also dates from this period.

The **Baroque** period covered the 17th and 18th centuries. In Milan, these were austere times, with the plague decimating the population and San Carlo Borromeo keeping a firm hand on the tiller. The best painting in these times came from Bergamo, Brescia and Mantua. The mid-18th century saw the emergence of two fine northern Italian painters, Alessandro Magnasco (1667–1749), who worked in Milan, and Giuseppe Bazzani (1690–1769) from Mantua. Architecturally, the period saw the construction in Milan of the Palazzo Reale and La Scala.

Italy made little contribution to art and architecture during the 19th century. One exception in Milan was the Galleria Vittorio Emanuele II, designed by Giuseppe Mengoni and something of an engineering triumph, making a it worthy neighbour of the Duomo. Some fine villas appeared around the shores of the Italian lakes during this period, many with superb gardens. Of the Italian artists of the time, the best known is Amedeo Modigliani (1884–1920), although he spent much of his working life in Paris.

ART IN MILAN

Visitors interested in art will find much to occupy their time in Milan. All the city's churches have frescoes to delight the eye, with the star exhibit being Leonardo di Vinci's *Last Supper* at the Church of Santa Maria delle Grazie (*see* page 36). There are a large number of art galleries, and few would want to miss the Pinacoteca di Brera, which holds one of Italy's most important collections and features work from the country's best-known artists. Enthusiasts of modern art should head for the Galleria d'Arte Moderna in Via Palestro.

Below: *The Italian lakes are lined with houses and villas displaying a variety of architecture. Many have their own boathouses.*

THE WORK OF GLACIERS

Glaciers are powerful agents of erosion and deposition and have had a tremendous effect on the scenery around the lakes. A glacier is able to erode the sheer weight of ice helped by the load of rocks carried within the ice. This is called abrasion. The rocks themselves are gradually worn down to smaller and smaller particles. This material is eventually deposited as low hills of moraine, which can block a valley and cause a lake to dam up behind it. Most of the northern Italian lakes, therefore, have been formed by a combination of erosion and deposition by glaciers.

During the early years of the 20th century, the Italian version of Art Nouveau, *Lo Stilo Liberty*, found its form in many of the hotels around the lakes. Mussolini's major contribution to architecture was the massive Stazione Centrale in Milan, which defies any stylistic definition. The post-World War II period saw Milan's first sky-scrapers, with the 1960 Pirelli Building remaining the pick of the bunch. In the early years of the century the art scene was enlivened by the Futurists, who glorified the new mechanistic age and attempted to drag Italian art into modern times. In latter years Milan's artistic endeavours seem to be in designing motor cars or making fashion statements rather than in fine art.

GOVERNMENT AND ECONOMY

Since 1946 Italy has been a democratic republic. Government takes place in Rome where the president is largely a figurehead. The decision-making is carried out by the lower house known as the Chamber of Deputies. The upper house consists of senators from the 21 different regions of Italy. The regions also have a measure of self-government. Each region is divided into provinces. The lowest level of government is the local council or *comune*.

Below: *The Italian flag has green, white and red vertical sections and is flown at all official functions.*

Voting

Every Italian is expected to vote as his civic duty, although there is no penalty for failing to do so. In fact, Italy has a higher turnout at election than any other European country – often over 90 per cent. The propor-

tional representation system and the large number of political parties in existence led to a vast number of coalition governments in the postwar period. The bargaining that went on fed the corruption that was endemic in Italian politics, so that in 1993 a new system was introduced whereby 75 per cent of the upper and lower houses were elected by the first-past-

the-post system, with the
remaining 25 per cent
elected by proportional
representation.

Political Parties

The strongest political
party in the postwar
years was the centre-right
Christian Democrats, who
usually shared power in a
coalition with three or four

other parties, thereby keeping out the communists. The
bribery and corruption scandals in recent years, and the
north's frustration with the backward south of the country, has spawned new parties known as *leghe* or leagues,
such as the Lega Nord, which are northern-based coalitions in favour of a federal Italy. Anti-Mafia parties have
also sprung up in the south. The two main parties, the
Christian Democrats and Socialists, have been almost
annihilated in recent elections, and new parties have
been formed such as Sylvio Berlusconi's centre-right
Forza Italia and the centre-left party of Romano Prodi.
The centre-left were in power in the late 1990s but were
defeated by Forza Italia in 2001.

The Economy

A grasp of the contrasts between the north and south of
Italy is essential in understanding the Italian economy.
The south of the peninsula is on the fringe of Europe,
with all the disadvantages of industrial location and
transportation. It is hot and dry and lacking in energy,
raw materials and resources. In addition it is dominated
by the Mafia whose influence extends into all parts of
daily life, preventing initiative, enterprise and investment.
In complete contrast, the north, based on the industrial
triangle of Milan, Turin and the port of Genoa, is the
powerhouse of the modern country. The climate is more
favourable for agriculture, and there are power sources in
the form of natural gas and hydroelectricity. Milan, itself

Above: *A funicular railway takes tourists to the
hill above Como.*

GAETANO DONIZETTI (1797–1848)

Donizetti was born in Bergamo
to a poor shopkeeping family.
His musical talent was soon
recognized, however, and he
gained a scholarship to study
at Bologna. His first opera
was performed when he was
25 and for many years he was
acknowledged as the leading
Italian opera composer.
Donizetti composed more
than 60 operas, including
Lucia di Lammermoor, *La
Figlia del Reggimento*, *La
Favorita* and *Don Pasquale*.
His fall from grace began in
1843 when the syphilis he
had caught in his youth
began to cause uncontrol-
lable fits of temper and
eventually madness. He
returned to Bergamo where
he died in 1848. His tomb,
with a fine memorial, is in
the church of Santa Maria
Maggiore, while his former
home in Via Arena is a rather
sad little museum.

with a population of around two million, is the country's economic capital. With its thriving industry, fashion houses, stock exchange and artistic heritage, it is a major European city. The Milanese and their fellow northerners feel that they are sub-sidizing the south, and there is frequent talk of federalism or even partition, but after a hard-won uni-fication campaign, this is unlikely to happen.

Above: *Senior citizens are respected and well provided for in northern Italy.*

THE PEOPLE

Language

Much of the Italian language is derived from Latin, so that visitors with a knowledge of French or Spanish will find the basics easy to pick up, particularly as each syllable is pronounced as it is seen and no letter is silent. There are vast numbers of regional dialects in Italy, and it was not until Dante wrote in the Tuscan dialect that this became the educated Italian to use. Some Italians even speak a different language, with German used in the Alto Adige region and French spoken in the Valle d'Aosta. The media, however, and particularly television, are gradually eliminating Italy's linguistic diversity.

Few Italians are good linguists, but the ability to speak good English confers some status. Visitors should find that in the tourist industry there will be someone in most of the hotels and restaurants who speaks English. Nevertheless, the ability to speak a few words of Italian will be greeted with smiles and pleasure.

Religion

The Roman Catholic church has been a dominant factor in Italian life for centuries and it still subtly permeates society today, although it no longer has the political

---

SENIOR CITIZENS IN NORTHERN ITALY

Elderly visitors will find that the Italian lakes are an ideal destination. The pace of life is slow and hotels and attractions are well prepared for the senior citizen. Pensioners will find that many concessions are available, such as lower entrance fees to museums and monuments. Be prepared, however, to produce proof of age.

power or social influence that it had in the past. Today, although 97 per cent of Italians are baptized and church marriages are the norm, fewer than 10 per cent regularly attend Mass. The strict rules of the past have been relaxed – both contraception and abortion are readily available, and the barriers to divorce have largely been removed. Despite this trend, the support for saints' days is undiminished, perhaps because all Italians enjoy a good party. Most saints' days involve a religious procession, when the statue of the saint is paraded through the streets. These are particularly atmospheric at Easter.

One of the pleasures of holidaying in northern Italy, however, is in visiting its cathedrals and churches. Few will be unimpressed by Milan's **Duomo**, the third largest cathedral in the world, and the city's clutch of ancient churches, many containing priceless works of art. The towns of the Italian lake region are also well endowed with historic churches, such as those at Como and Bergamo. (Visitors should remember that beachwear and shorts are not considered appropriate dress in churches.)

> **A CHILD-FRIENDLY COUNTRY**
>
> Do not worry about taking babies or young children to the Italian lakes, as they will be made very welcome. Children keep very late nights and are not excluded from any family activities. Waiters traditionally make a huge fuss of small children who come to their restaurants and will prepare special portions for them. Older children will find plenty to occupy themselves and will enjoy the theme parks and boat trips.

The Family

The family has always been a major influence in Italian life, probably due to the country's agricultural past and the need for cooperation in order to survive, plus the teachings of the Catholic church. Today, children, particularly males, tend to live at home until their thirties. Most students attend their local university and continue to reside at home, maintaining the traditional link between mother and son. In Italy the matriarchal structure is alive and well!

The north of Italy has seen a weakening of the family structure in recent decades, due to social changes such as the lower birth rate, the availability of divorce, and geographical migration in search of work. In the south, however, the family is as strong as ever.

Below: *A skilfully carved door – typical of the rich artwork in the churches of northern Italy.*

REGIONAL DIFFERENCES IN COOKING

The social and economic differences between the north and south of Italy are very noticeable. The comparison extends to cooking. Pasta in the north of Italy tends to be the flat variety, freshly made with eggs, whereas in the south the tubular varieties of pasta are more usual. In the north, the fat used for cooking is generally butter, while in the south olive oil is more popular. Flavours, particularly in sauces, are much stronger in the south, where full use is made of the Mediterranean aromatic herbs such as rosemary and thyme.

Food and Drink

Although few people would actually choose a holiday in northern Italy because of its food, one of the joys of visiting the area is to sample its cuisine and its wines. To be precise there is no such thing as typically Italian food, because there are a vast number of regional variations. Another popular misconception is that Italian food is all pasta and pizza. These do, of course, figure prominently on menus, but there are also some fine regional fish and meat dishes.

Food

Although many hotels provide an international-style **breakfast**, the average Milanese does not make a big thing about this meal, which is likely to be a quick coffee and a *brioche* taken standing at a bar.

Lunch, however, is a different matter. Many workers will take a long lunch with four courses (although others will prefer to have a light lunch and save the big meal for the evening). The meal starts with the *antipasti* (literally 'before the pasta'). Similar to the French hors d'oeuvres, *antipasti* may be served buffet-style on a long table, often placed near the door of the restaurant to tempt diners in. Here a variety of items are on offer, including seafood, hams, mushrooms and salad from which you can make up your own assortment, known as *antipasto mista*.

The second course is known, confusingly, as the *primo piatto*. A soup is always on offer and this will either be a thick country soup or a thin minestrone on which Parmesan cheese can be sprinkled. As the Lombardy Plain is a rice-growing area, a risotto is an alternative choice. These are often coloured yellow with saffron and may come with vegetables, meat or seafood. The third choice will involve pasta. There are said to be over 350 pasta shapes, but the most common are spaghetti, tagliatelle, lasagna, the meat-stuffed ravioli, and cannelloni. There are almost as many sauces to accompany the pasta, while Parmesan cheese is usually offered as a topping. Don't expect the waiter to come around with an enormous pepper grinder – this only happens in Italian restaurants abroad!

Below: *Pasta comes in a vast variety of forms, often with imaginative sauces.*

The main course is the *secondo piatto* and will be a meat or fish dish accompanied by a modicum of potatoes and vegetables. Regional specialities include *Cotoletta alla Milanese*, which is a veal slice dipped in egg and fried in breadcrumbs. Chicken (*pollo*), pork

(*maiale*), beef (*manzo*) and lamb (*agnello*) are other meat choices. Another local speciality for those with strong stomachs is *busecca*, which is tripe with white beans. The fish is likely to be of the freshwater variety from the lakes to the north, and could include carp, trout or perch. Among the seafood, sea bass (*spigola*), red mullet (*triglia*) and swordfish (*pesce spada*) are often on the menu.

To complete the meal there will **cheese**, **desserts** or **fresh fruit**. Apart from the well-known blue-veined *gorgonzola* and *bel paese*, there is a whole host of local cheeses from all over the country. Italian desserts can be a delight or a disappointment, but you cannot go wrong with Italian ice cream, particularly in Milan, which considers itself a specialist ice cream making area.

Visitors preferring a pizza should head for one of the specialist **pizzerias**, where the food is cooked in the traditional oven. The pizzas are usually thin and cooked to age-old recipes – don't expect any exotic toppings such as sweet corn or pineapple.

Above: *A visit to an Italian market is a highly recommended holiday experience.*

Drinks

Italy produces more wine than any other country in the world and much of it is from the Lombardy area. Probably the best-known wines are the light red (*rossi*) Valpollicellas and Bardolinos and the crisp white (*bianco*) Soaves grown to the east and south of Lake Garda. To the west of Lake Maggiore are the good quality red wines that include the full-bodied Barolo and the fragrant Barbaresco. Much of the wine exported from

---

NORTHERN SPECIALITIES

Two northern products that are known worldwide are **prosciutto ham** and **Parmesan cheese**, which both come from the Parma area to the southeast of Milan. Parmesan cheese is left for two years to dry and mature and becomes stronger with age. The whey from the cheese is fed to the local pigs. Ham is carefully dried and salted to give the delicately flavoured prosciutto. The region's products clearly bring profit – it is claimed that Parma has the highest standard of living of any city in Italy!

Above: *Among the many Italian spirits is the daunting* grappa.

northern Italy in the past has been of only moderate standard but in more recent years higher quality wines have been produced. It is a good idea to try local wines – ask for *vino locale* or *vino della casa*. The Italians are certainly not wine snobs and frequently keep their lighter red wines in the fridge during the summer. Often their stronger white wines are not chilled at all.

Fortified wines include the usual *cinzano*, *martini* and *campari*. A wide variety of **spirits** are on sale. A popular local fire-water is *grappa*, which is drunk for effect rather than taste. Good local brandies include *stock* and *Vecchia Romagna*. Widely drunk **liqueurs** include *strega* (often taken with ice), the apricot-flavoured *amaretto*, cherry *marascino* and the aniseed-tasting *sambuca*.

Beer (*birra*) comes in bottles or draught and is of the lager type. A small bottle is a *pícola* and a larger bottle is known as a *media*. There are also darker beers available. Known as *birra nera*, they are sweeter and heavier and resemble English bitter. The local beers include Peroni, Moretti and Dreher, which are all excellent. If you don't ask for them you will probably be given foreign imported beers, which will be more expensive.

There are plenty of **soft drinks** to choose from, including a wide variety of fruit juices. Fizzy drinks include the ubiquitous cola and the thirst-quenching lemon soda. Tap water is usually drinkable, but the Italians themselves drink vast amounts of bottled mineral water (*aqua minerale*), which comes either sparkling (*con gas*) or still (*naturale*).

Tea and Coffee

The Italians are enthusiastic coffee drinkers, and it comes in a bewildering variety. It is always made in an espresso machine – instant coffee is rarely an option. The choice is usually between a small black *espresso* or a larger white *cappuccino* (don't expect a topping of chocolate grains). Other possibilities are a longer, weaker coffee (*Americana*),

---

WINE FACTS

Wine has been grown in Italy for more than 3000 years, so we need not be surprised that Italians are the greatest wine drinkers in the world, consuming 82 litres (143 pints) per capita per year. Italy also produces more wine than any other country – a massive 77 million hectolitres (1,700,000,000 gallons) annually, comprising a quarter of world production. Italy is also the only country in the world where vines can be grown in every region in the land.

a long coffee with a dash of milk (*macchiato*), and a long milky coffee (*latte*). Many Italians like a drop of spirit in their drink – this is called *caffè corretto*. A popular choice in summer is to take coffee cold (*caffè freddo*). If it is topped with crushed ice and cream, you have *caffè granita*.

Tea (*tè*) is much simpler. It comes either with lemon (*con limone*) or milk (*con latte*), but in summer cold tea (*tè freddo*) is also popular.

Sport and Recreation

Of the spectator sports, **football** (*calcio*) is almost like a religion. The Italian League is divided into four divisions, the most prestigious of which is called Serie A. Matches are played in the winter months, usually on Saturday afternoons at the San Siro Stadium (*see* page 47). Other popular spectator sports have been imported from America and include **basketball** and **baseball**. Also keenly followed is **motor racing**, and an annual Grand Prix is held at Monza just north of Milan. **Cycling**, too, is popular with both riders and spectators, and the weekend roads are full of recreational and competitive cyclists.

Northern Italy and the lakes provide a venue for a number of recreational activities. There is a long **skiing** season in the Alps, which can easily be reached from Milan. In the summer the mountains are popular for **hiking** and **rock climbing**. The lakes are used for a variety of water sports. The northern end of Lake Garda is one of the world's prime **windsurfing** locations and it also provides challenging sailing conditions. **Canoeing** has boomed in recent years, particularly on the whitewater stretches of the rivers leading into the lakes.

Personal fitness is not something that interests the majority of Italians, but a number of fitness and leisure centres have recently sprung up in Milan. Here it is very important to look good and the leisure centre gives the opportunity to show off the latest designer sportswear.

WATER SPORTS ON THE LAKES

The Italian lakes provide plenty of opportunity for water sports. There are a number of shingle beaches that provide safe **swimming** and **snorkelling**. Many types of craft can be hired, from **pedaloes** to **jet skis**, while **water-skiing** is popular in many areas. The northern parts of the lakes are often windy and are ideal for **sailing**. The northern end of Lake Garda is one of the prime **windsurfing** areas in Europe.

Below: *Sunday morning is the traditional time for chess in Bergamo Alta's main square.*

2
Milan

It has been said that 'anyone who understands Milan understands Italy'. Milan is a microcosm of Italian life, far more so than sleepy Florence, historic Rome or picture postcard Venice. Milan is Italy's industrial and commercial capital, its second largest city, a world centre for fashion and high finance, and the focus of the country's media. It is, however, more than just a business city – its historic core, centred on the Duomo or cathedral, boasts a fine collection of medieval churches, art galleries, museums and palaces.

Milan has an atmosphere more akin to a northern European city, rather than the somnolent south of Italy. A long afternoon siesta is considered a waste of time, for the Milanese are too busy making money. Milan's traditional industries include vehicles, textiles, clothing and chemicals, but in recent years the service industries have become dominant. This industrial success has drawn immigrants, not only from southern Italy, but from many parts of the world, including Africa and Asia. Milan has always been a melting pot for other cultures and today the recent immigrants give the city a cosmopolitan feel. Although central Milan has lost population in recent years, its metropolitan district has grown enormously and it is estimated that nearly half a million people commute into the city daily, putting a great strain on the transport services and causing congestion on the roads.

Milan's inhabitants may work hard but they also know how to enjoy their leisure. The city has 50 cinemas, almost as many theatres and some of the best discos and

DON'T MISS

*** The Duomo: Milan's magnificent Gothic cathedral.
*** Castello Sforzesco: the stronghold of the dynastic Visconti and Sforza families.
*** Santa Maria delle Grazie: the church displays da Vinci's *Last Supper*.
** Galleria Vittorio Emanuele II: 19th-century shopping arcade.
** The Brera: one of Italy's finest art galleries.
** Via Monte Napoleone: main street of the Quadrilatero d'Oro, where famous fashion designers have their shops.

Opposite: *Milan's Duomo, where a lift takes visitors to the roof for a view of the city.*

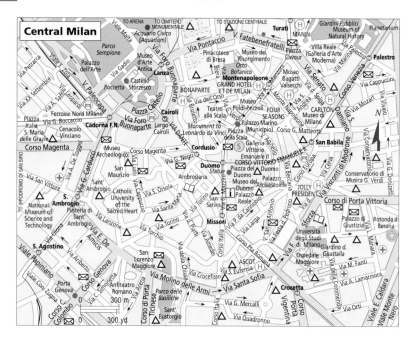

Central Milan

MILAN'S CLIMATE

The average January temperature in Milan is 1.9°C (35°F)
and winters can be raw.
Precipitation is light, but
there is some snowfall in
most years. Fog can linger
for days on end. The average
July temperature is 24.8°C
(76°F) and it is even higher in
August, when the humidity
can be trying. Thunderstorms
can be expected in late
summer. May and September
are the most pleasant months
for sightseeing.

nightclubs in the country. During weekends, the Milanese
stream out northwards to the lakes, where many of the
city's flat-dwellers have villas and boats.

Milan's road system, which is a combination of con-
centric ring roads and radiating avenues, owes much to its
ancient past. The inner ring road (*convallazione interna*)
encloses much of the medieval city, where most of the
historic sights can be seen. The 19th-century industry
extended out to the canal ring (*cerchia dei navigli*), which
has largely been filled in. Postwar development has spread
towards the outer ring road (*circunvallazione esterna*). Most
visitors, however, spend their time in the historic core,
where most of Milan's attractions can be reached on foot.

PIAZZA DEL DUOMO

The heart of Milan is the Piazza del Duomo, or Cathedral
Square (Metro 1, 3, Duomo). It is always throbbing with
activity, with tourists feeding the pigeons and taking

photographs, businessmen striding purposefully towards their offices, and the youth of Milan simply hanging out with their friends. Surrounding the square is a fine array of 19th-century arcaded buildings with their ground floors providing welcome cafés. On the north side of the square is the neo-Renaissance **Galleria Vittorio Emanuele II**, while on the south side is the rather ugly **Palazzo dell' Argengario**, which is now the conveniently sited **tourist office** (open 08:00–19:00 Monday–Saturday; tel 02 7252 4300). At the western end of the square is the bronze equestrian **Statue of Victor Emmanuel II**, the work of Ercole Rosa, which was unveiled in 1896. The statue depicts the king at the Battle of San Martino in 1859, while the sides of the massive plinth show the triumphant entry of the Piedmont troops into Milan after the Battle of Magenta (1859). The only jarring note about the piazza is the western end, where commercial buildings covered with neon advertisements somewhat ruin the atmosphere. This area is due for redevelopment, so hopefully improvements are on the way. One aspect of the Piazza del Duomo that the visitor will **not** see – because it underground – is the remains of the Basilica of St Tecla, which was unearthed during an archaeological dig in 1942.

The Duomo ★★★

Dominating the piazza, of course, is the Duomo or cathedral. As you emerge from the metro, you have a breathtaking view of the west front, with its pink-fringed marble and forest of pinnacles and statues. The sheer size of the cathedral is also impressive. It is claimed that the Duomo is the third largest cathedral in the world after Seville in Spain and St Peter's in Rome. It is also the only Gothic cathedral of any note in Italy.

The Duomo was begun in 1386 by Gian Galeazzo Visconti. The cathedral itself took another 500 years to complete. The main spire, with its golden Madonna, was added in the 18th century, and it was left to Napoleon to complete the west façade in 1813. Even in the 20th century, work was being carried out on the roof and the five bronze doors on the façade.

FACTS ABOUT THE DUOMO

Length: 158m (520ft).
Width: 66m (215ft).
Central nave: 17m (55ft) wide; 48m (157ft) high.
Interior height of dome: 68m (220ft).
Distance from statue of the Madonna to the ground: 108m (355ft).
Main façade: 66m (200ft) wide; 56m (180ft) high.
Tallest spire: 108m (355ft) high.
There are 135 **spires**, 2245 statues, and 96 **gargoyles**.

Below: *In the Piazza del Duomo this imposing equestrian statue of Victor Emmanuel II faces the cathedral.*

**THE NAIL OF
THE HOLY CROSS**

Stand in the choir of the
Duomo and look up into the
vaulting. A small red light
marks a niche that contains
a nail reputed to come from
Christ's cross. The nail is in
the shape of a horseshoe and
was found by St Helena. It
eventually came into the pos-
session of Sant'Ambrogio.
San Carlo Borromeo carried
the nail in the procession
during the plague of 1576.
Each September 14, the
Bishop of Milan is carried
heavenwards on a small plat-
form with invisible pulleys (it
must seem like a miracle!) to
collect the nail and show it to
the people of Milan.

The most photographed part of the Duomo is the ornate west front or **façade**. Six huge vertical buttresses divide this triangular shape into five sections, each of which is capped with a range of pinnacles.

The initial impression on entering the **interior** is one of gloom, but on becoming accustomed to the light it is apparent that there are five aisles supported by 52 pillars (said to represent the weeks of the year). The capitals on each pillar are, unusually, decorated with statues of the saints. The exceptional stained glass varies in age from 15th century to modern, and casts a delicate light.

Let us take an anticlockwise walk around the interior of the cathedral. On the floor at the west end is a **meridian** placed there by the Brera astronomers in 1786. Along the south aisle you can appreciate the stunning stained glass. In the north transept there is a gruesome **Statue of St Bartholomew**. Dating from 1562, it shows the saint, having been flayed alive, carrying his own skin!

Walk over towards the altar and take the door that leads down to the **crypt**. For a small entrance charge admittance is gained to the room where an octagonal Baroque vault contains the remains of San Carlo Borromeo, the 16th-century Bishop of Milan. Returning to ground level, walk along the choir aisle, noting the funerary **Monument to Gian Giacomo Medici**. At this stage look at the vault above the choir where a small red light marks the niche where a nail from Christ's cross is kept.

Entering the ambulatory, don't miss the **southern sacristy door**, which dates from 1393 and has some superb carvings and inscriptions. You now reach the **apse**, which is generally considered to be the most beautiful part of the cathedral. There are

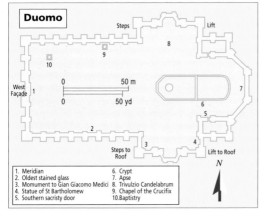

three magnificent windows with delicate tracery and some fine 19th-century glass. The ambulatory now leads to the north transept, which is dominated by the monumental early 13th-century **Trivulzio Candelabrum**, attributed to French goldsmith Nicholas de Verdun. The enormous

4.87m (16ft) candelabrum has seven branches and sits on a decorated stone base.

Returning along the north aisle, you pass the **Chapel of the Crucifix**, which contains the nail that San Carlo Borromeo carried in a procession to thwart the plague of 1576 (*see* panel, page 32). The route has now returned to the west end. Before leaving, take the steps down to the octagonal **baptistry** where Sant'Ambrogio is reputed to have baptized St Augustine in AD387.

A tour of the Duomo would not be complete without a visit to the **roof terraces**. Fortunately, the vast number of stairs can be avoided by using the lift (small charge) on the north side of the cathedral. The roof gives an opportunity to study the statues, spires and buttresses in detail. There are also fine views over the city's rooftops and it is even possible, on a clear day, to see the Alps in the distance.

Palazzo Reale ★★

Just to the southeast of the Duomo is the Palazzo Reale, a building with a chequered history. When Milan was a *comune* in the 11th and 12th centuries, the Palazzo was the town hall. Later it was the seat of the Visconti family, but when the front part of the building was removed to make way for the cathedral, the Dukes of Milan moved to the Castello Sforzesco. The palace later became the residence of both the Spanish and Austrian governors. After unification, the building was renamed the Palazzo Reale (Royal Palace). It was handed over to the city authorities in the 20th century.

Above: *Palazzo Reale was once the seat of the Visconti family.*

MILAN'S ASTOUNDING POPULATION GROWTH

Earliest population figures available show that from the 13th to 15th centuries Milan had a population of around 200,000, making it the largest city in Europe. At the time of the 1630 plague the figure had dropped right down to 60,000. Thereafter there was a gradual recovery until the end of the 19th century when there was a massive spurt in population numbers. By 1923 it had reached 850,000, and in the post-World War II period it neared 1,400,000, making Milan the second largest city in Italy and 10th largest in Europe. Greater Milan today has 3,780,000 inhabitants. What has caused this startling growth? The answer is **economic migration**. Milan's thriving industry has attracted migrants looking for work from many areas of southern Italy and other parts of the world including North Africa and Asia.

Above: *The Galleria Vittorio Emanuele II, built in the late 19th century, is a stylish shopping arcade.*

WHAT'S IN A NAME?

How did Milan get its name? The obvious answer is that it derives from either the Celtic 'midland' or the Roman *Mediolanum*, meaning 'in the middle of the plain' – Milan lies in the middle of the Plain of Lombardy between the Alps and the Apennines. Some authorities, however, claim that the name comes from *scrofa semilanuta*, the half-woolly bear, which was the city's emblem in pre-Roman times.

Civico Museo d'Arte Contemporanea (CIMAC) *

The second floor of the Palazzo Reale houses Milan's modern art museum. It has a fine collection of paintings and sculptures, including work by Klee, Picasso, Modigliani and Matisse. Open 10:00–13:00 and 14:30–18:30 Monday, Wednesday–Friday; 10:30–18:30 Saturday and Sunday; closed on Tuesday.

Museo del Duomo **

(Metro 1, 3, Duomo)

A wing of the Palazzo Reale is occupied by the Museo del Duomo. Among its collections are paintings, sculptures, stained-glass windows and a host of religious objects from the cathedral. A star exhibit is a wooden model of the Duomo dating from 1519. The Museo del Duomo is open from 09:30–12:30 and 15:00–18:00; closed on Monday.

The Galleria Vittorio Emanuele II ***

(Metro 1, 3, Duomo)

This stylish shopping arcade has four 'arms', the south and north arms connecting the Piazza del Duomo with the Piazza della Scala. The Galleria was built between 1865 and 1877 to the design of Giuseppe Mengoni, who sadly fell to his death from scaffolding shortly before the arcade was opened. The Galleria is entered through a squat 'triumphal arch', which leads to the central dome, made of iron and glass, and considered to be an engineering triumph in its day. The Galleria is claimed to be the most exclusive shopping arcade in the country and is filled with fashion outlets, bookshops and restaurants. The elite of Milan like to be seen eating here after attending a performance at La Scala. Beneath the dome is Il Savini, considered to be the most exclusive restaurant in Milan. Amazingly, the diners at Il Savini have to look across to an American fast-food chain – an unfortunate juxtaposition.

PIAZZA DELLA SCALA

The north arm of the Galleria leads into the Piazza della Scala. In the centre of the square is Pietro Magni's **Monument to Leonardo da Vinci**, erected in 1872. On the corners of the plinth are Leonardo's pupils, Boltraffio, Salaino, Oggiono and da Sesto. Between their figures are reliefs showing the various fields of work in which Leonardo excelled – anatomy, hydraulic engineering, painting and architecture. Between the monument and Galleria lies the **Palazzo Marino**, a 16th-century building, now the City Hall.

La Scala ***

(Metro 1, 3, Duomo)
On the other side of the square, opposite Palazzo Marino, is the world's most famous opera house – **La Scala**. The name is derived from the Church of Santa Maria alla Scala that once stood on the site. The opera house was financed by the Austrian Empress Maria Theresa and opened in 1778. All the world's best-known conductors and opera singers have performed at La Scala. Unfortunately, at the time of writing, La Scala is closed for renovations and not expected to re-open until 2005.

Museo la Scala **

The museum is normally located just to the left of the main doors of La Scala, but while the opera house is closed, the museum can be found in temporary quarters in the Palazzo Busca, at corso Magenta 71. There is a fascinating collection of opera memorabilia, including musical

> **ALL THE WORLD'S A STAGE**
>
> The stage at La Scala Opera House is one of the largest in the world, measuring 1200m² (13,000 sq ft). Beneath the stage is the orchestra pit. Until 1907 the orchestra had played on the same level as the stalls. The large stage also accommodates the theatre's *corps de ballet*, many of whose members come from La Scala's Ballet School.

**GIUSEPPE VERDI
(1813–1901)**

Born in Parma, Verdi moved
to Milan at a very early age
and spent most of his life in
the city. He failed to gain
entrance to the conservatoire,
which ironically now bears
his name. He is known almost
entirely for his operas, most
of which had their debuts
at La Scala. They included
Rigoletto (1851), *La Traviata*
(1853), *Aïda* (1871) and
Otello (1887). Verdi made his
home in the Grand Hotel et
de Milan, where he died in
what is now suite 107.

scores, sets, and paintings of several famous performers.
The museum is open from 09:00–12:00 and 14:00–18:00
daily. Closed on Monday.

Church of Santa Maria delle Grazie ***
(Metro 1, 2, Cadorna; 1, Conciliazione)

Few visitors to Milan would wish to miss the opportunity to see Leonardo da Vinci's painting of the *Last
Supper*. Head for the Church of Santa Maria delle Grazie.
Da Vinci's masterpiece is in the refectory, but first look
around the church. The exterior is largely brick and is
distinguished by the hemispherical dome on a cubic
base. Santa Maria delle Grazie was built between 1463
and 1490 by Guiniforte Solari in a style described as a
'Gothic Renaissance transitional'. Ludovico el Moro later
commissioned Bramante to make alterations, and the
architect replaced the original apse with one in
Renaissance style. Find time to visit the charming Great
and Little Cloisters. The latter leads to the sacristy, which
is often used today for art exhibitions.

The refectory, which contains the **Last Supper**, is
entered by a separate door and an admission fee is
charged. It is open from 08:00–14:00 Tuesday–Saturday;
09:00–19:30 Sunday; closed on Monday. Times are notoriously variable and it is highly unlikely that you will gain
immediate entry. You may even have to wait for the next
day. It is advisable, therefore, to book ahead by telephone
(1 euro booking fee) on 02 8942 1146. The *Last Supper* was
painted by Leonardo for Ludovico el Moro between 1495
and 1497, and covers the entire rear wall of the refectory,
measuring 9m (30ft) by 4.5m (14ft). It depicts the moment

Below: *La Scala, the
world-famous opera house,
was named after a 14th-
century church that once
occupied the site.*

just after Christ said: 'One of you will
betray me'. The painting began to de-
teriorate almost immediately and it has
had some controversial restoration over
the centuries. Don't dismiss the painting
on the opposite wall of the refectory.
This is Donato da Montafano's
Crucifixion, which dates from 1495 and
was commissioned by the Dominicans.

National Museum of Science and Technology ★★

(Metro 2, Sant'Ambrogio)

Just a stone's throw from Santa Maria delle Grazie is another location for da Vinci fans – the National Museum of Science and Technology. It is housed in the

Above: *Da Vinci's* Last Supper, *on the refectory wall of the Church of Santa Maria delle Grazie.*

16th-century Monastery of San Vittore, which, after the monasteries were suppressed, became a military hospital and later a barracks. Badly damaged during World War II, it was restored soon afterwards and became the museum in 1947. The collections occupy a number of buildings, and there are sections on transport, metallurgy, physics, optics, acoustics, printing, cinema photography and astronomy. The **Leonardo da Vinci Gallery** attracts people by the score and his inventions are well displayed. There is a Leonardo self-portrait engraved on a glass panel, and a room dedicated to his drawings and models, some of which can be worked by visitors. The museum is open 09:30–16:50 Tuesday–Friday; 09:30–18:30 on Saturday; closed on Monday.

THE CASTELLO SFORZESCO AREA

(Metro 1, Cairoli-Cadorna; 2, Lanza-Cadorna)

To the northwest of the Duomo the pedestrianized Via Dante, with its open-air cafés, leads to the Largo Cairoli, a large square ringed by distinguished 19th-century buildings. In the centre of the square is an equestrian statue of Giuseppe Garibaldi by Ettore Ximenes, erected in 1895. From here the tree-lined Via Foro Buonaparte stretches in a semicircle around the Piazza Castello and the Castello Sforzesco.

Castello Sforzesco ★★★

This complex of brick buildings and towers, which in the past formed a formidable defensive fortress, now contains a series of excellent museums.

The castle has a long and fascinating history. It was built in 1368 by the Viscontis purely as a fortress, but

PAINTING THE LAST SUPPER

Fresco is a technique where the paint is put onto 'fresh' (*fresco*) mortar, which in drying binds the coloured pigment so that the painting becomes part of the wall itself. When Leonardo painted the *Last Supper* he tried a different technique, using tempera over a double layer of plaster. This proved faulty as the fresco could not withstand the dampness of the wall it was painted on and very soon it began to decay. Experts have tried heating the wall from behind, but this was unsuccessful. The fresco has been 'restored' so many times over the centuries that it is highly probable that little of Leonardo's original paintwork survives.

Above: *Statues and other works of art abound at the Castello Sforzesco.*

THE EDICT OF MILAN

In AD313 in Milan the Emperor Constantine made a proclamation granting religious tolerance for Christianity within the Roman Empire. The Edict assured Christians of their legal rights and directed the prompt return of their confiscated property. As a result of the Edict, Milan became the capital of western Christendom. A bronze statue of the Emperor Constantine (a copy of a Roman original) can be seen in the courtyard of the Basilica of San Lorenzo, fittingly located between the church's portals and the line of Roman columns. It is, however, doubtful whether Constantine himself ever became a Christian, although the Church claimed that he was baptized on his deathbed.

later became the ducal palace. During the short-lived Ambrosian Republic it was partially demolished, but rebuilt almost immediately by the Sforzas. Under Ludovico el Moro it evolved into a glittering Renaissance palace, in which Leonardo da Vinci and Bramante the architect worked. During the times of Spanish and Austrian occupation it reverted to the role of fortress. It was badly damaged during the Napoleonic era, but restored to its original 15th-century magnificence by Luca Beltrami in the 1890s. The castle was further damaged by bombs during World War II, necessitating more restoration in the postwar years.

The castle takes the shape of a square, with massive walls pockmarked with holes at regular intervals. Once used for scaffolding, they now provide homes for some of Milan's ubiquitous pigeons. The main façade facing the Largo Cairoli has a round tower at each corner. These towers reach 31m (100ft) high and show the emblem of the snake, the symbol of the Sforza and Visconti families. Once water cisterns, the towers were given a military makeover in Beltrami's reconstructions. In the centre of the façade is the **Filarete Tower**, named after its designer. In 1521, it collapsed when the gunpowder that was stored there exploded. Beltrami rebuilt it from Filarete's original plans.

Pass the ornate computerized fountain and enter the main gateway under the Filarete Tower. This leads into the enormous Piazza D'Armi, the Sforza military training ground. Cross this courtyard and pass through a gateway. To the right is the Ducal Court containing the **Sforza Castle art galleries**. The first of these is the **Civic Museum of Art**, which is mainly given over to sculpture and tapestries. The prize exhibit is Michelangelo's *Rondanini Pietà*. The unfinished sculpture shows Mary struggling to hold up the body of the crucified Christ. On the other side of the courtyard in the upper storey is the **Pinacoteca**, which has a comprehensive collection of art from the 15th–18th centuries, including work by Bellini, Titian, Canaletto and a number of Lombard artists.

On the opposite side of the castle is the arcaded **Roccetta Courtyard**, which was always the last refuge in the event of a siege. The museum here has a collection of ancient Egyptian artefacts and local archaeological items. The castle is open 09:00–17:30 daily and the museums 09:00–17:30 Tuesday–Sunday. Free admission.

Continuing through the castle and over the moat, you reach the **Parco Sempione**. Once the Sforza family's hunting grounds, the park was remodelled in the late 19th century by Emilio Alemagna in what was considered to be typically English style. Today, the park covers about 47ha (116 acres) and includes a number of lakes between the mature trees. Almost hidden among this leafiness is the **Monument to Napoleon III**, dating from 1881 and brought here in 1927 from its original site at the Senate building. Nearby is the **Acquario Civico**, which has a good collection of mammals and fish. It is very popular with Italian schoolchildren. The aquarium is open 09:30–17:30 daily.

On the opposite side of the park is the **Palazzo dell' Arte**. Built in 1933, it is the permanent venue for the Milan Triennale, and occasionally stages other exhibitions of art, fashion and design.

At the far end of the park is the **Arco della Pace**. Standing 25m (82ft) high, its construction began in 1807 as a triumphal arch in celebration of Napoleon's victories. On Napoleon's fall from power, work stopped on the arch and it was not resumed until 1826, when Francis I of Austria dedicated it to Peace.

> **THE EMPEROR WITHOUT HIS CLOTHES**
>
> Dominating the cobbled courtyard of the Brera Art Gallery is a bronze statue of Napoleon. This is fitting, as the Emperor was responsible for setting up the gallery. However, this is no ordinary statue of Napoleon – it is a nude Napoleon! Antonio Canova's bronze statue was executed in 1809. The emperor was middle-aged when he conquered Milan and he is depicted here as a nude young god, holding a sceptre in his right hand and a personification of victory in his left hand.

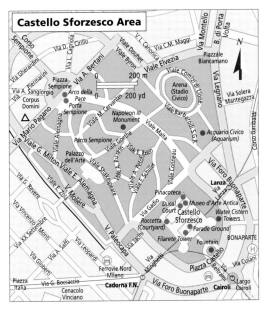

Castello Sforzesco Area

ALESSANDRO MANZONI
(1785–1873)

One of Milan's most famous residents, Manzoni wrote what is considered to be Italy's greatest novel, *I Promessi Sposi* (The Betrothed), describing life in Milan in the 17th century. In the novel he used a form of Italian that everyone could understand, stirring feelings for unification. His former home, **Casa Manzoni**, in Via Morone, is now a museum and the seat of the National Centre for Manzoni Studies. The house also contains the Lombard History Society's collection of over 40,000 books.

Below: *The Milan fashion shows are renowned the world over.*

THE BRERA QUARTER
(Metro 1, 3, Duomo; 2, Lanza)

The Brera area is one of the liveliest and most atmospheric parts of Milan. The winding, cobbled streets are full of cafés, art galleries and antique shops, while students from the Academy of Fine Art add to the colourful ambience. A good time to visit the quarter is on the third Saturday of each month when a flea market is held in the Via Brera.

Pinacoteca di Brera ★★★

The focus for most visitors to the Brera area will be the Pinacoteca di Brera, one of Italy's top art galleries. It is located in a palace that dates from 1773, although it is on the site of a much earlier monastery. Entry is via a rectangular courtyard with a double arcade of slender paired columns. In the centre of the cobbled courtyard is a bronze statue of Napoleon, who was largely responsible for getting together the original collection from suppressed churches. The collection has since been augmented by donations. The paintings are mainly Italian and 90 per cent of those displayed are of a religious nature. Particularly important are Bramante's eight frescoes, Tintoretto's *Rediscovery of St Mark's Body*, the *Pietà* by Bellini, several Raphaels including *The Marriage of the Virgin*, and *Virgin With Child* by Piero della Francesca. Don't miss the foreshortened *Dead Christ* by Mantegna. The gallery is on the first floor and reached by the steps from the courtyard. The Brera is open 09:00–19:30 Tuesday–Saturday; 09:00–12:30 Sunday; closed on Monday.

THE FASHION DISTRICT
(Metro 1, Duomo)

Via Monte Napoleone, Via Manzoni, Via Sant'Andrea and Via della Spiga enclose the Quadrilatero d'Oro, Milan's famous fashion district. Here are the shops of some of the top international fashion designers interspersed with aristocratic palaces, tearooms and antique shops. Names such as Armani, Gucci, Versace, Chanel and Cardin ensure that this district is a Mecca for serious shoppers and spenders.

Just to the northeast of the fashion district are the **Giardini Pubblici**, Milan's public gardens. They cover some 17ha (42 acres) and were originally laid out in 1782 by Piermarini, who used the grounds of suppressed monasteries. Within the public gardens are the city's **Planetarium** (open according to the programme with guided tours) and the **Museum of Natural History**, which has a good collection of fossils (including dinosaurs), minerals and insects. Open 09:00–18:00 Monday–Friday; 09:30–18:30 on Saturday and Sunday.

Above: *Magnificent window displays can be found in the Quadrilatero d'Oro.*

CA' GRANDE

(Metro 1, 3, Duomo; 3, Missori)
Southeast of the Duomo is the Casa Grande or Ospedale Maggiore. This former hospital was built in the mid-15th century for Francesco Sforza, who planned to centralize the city's many hospitals. It has a magnificent arcaded central courtyard, which separated the men's and women's quarters. Since 1952 Ca' Grande has been the home of the Liberal Arts faculty of Milan's State University.

OTHER MUSEUM HIGHLIGHTS

There are over 50 museums and galleries in Milan. Some have already been described. Here is the pick of the remainder. Remember that most museums are closed on Sunday afternoons and all day on Monday. In theory all state museums should be free to all EU citizens under 18 and over 65 – but in practice this may not be the case.

FASHION AND FRAUD

Anyone strolling around the Quadrilatero d'Oro – the Golden Quadrangle – will have little doubt that Milan regards itself as the fashion capital of the world. Not only are there shops with household names such as Versace, Gucci, Armani, Benetton and many more, but the Italians strolling around the street dress themselves in the latest fashion. The Milanese like to *fare bella figura* or cut a fine figure – even the local footballers look like male models. Unfortunately the fashion world was caught up in the fraud and corruption allegations of the 1990s, and two of the leading figures have been assassinated – Gianni Versace in Florida and Maurizio Gucci in Milan.

Above: *The Milan metro is cheap, effective and the best way to get around the city.*

Museo Poldi Pezzoli *

(Metro 3, Montenapoleone)

Located on Via Manzoni, this museum is only a short walk from the Piazza della Scala. As well as some highly regarded artwork including paintings by Mantegna, Bellini and Canaletto, there are displays of glassware, clocks, porcelain and tapestry. Open 09:30–12:30 and 14:20–18:00 Tuesday–Saturday; 09:30–12:30 Sunday; closed on Monday.

Museo Archeologico *

(Metro 1, 2, Cadorna)

Based in a former monastery located at corso Magenta 15, the archaeological museum has some interesting collections from prehistoric, Etruscan and Roman times. Open 09:30–17:30; closed on Monday.

Ambrosiana **

(Metro 1, 3, Duomo; 1, Cordusio)

On Piazza Pio XI – just to the west of the Duomo – the Ambrosiana is a huge library and art gallery, set up by Federico Borromeo, cousin of the better-known bishop. The library contains over 750,000 books and priceless manuscripts, including some of Leonardo's sketchbooks. The superb art collection includes Leonardo's *Portrait of a Musician*, Caravaggio's impression of a basket of worm-eaten fruit (thought to be the first still life painted in Italy), and works by Tintoretto, Botticelli and Titian. Open 10:00–17:30; closed on Monday.

Pusterla di Sant'Ambrogio *

(Metro 3, Duomo)

Set in one of the medieval city gates at via Carducci 41, the museum has a collection of ancient weapons and criminological artefacts. Open 10:00–13:00 and 15:00–19:00 daily; closed on Monday.

USING THE METRO

Using Milan's underground railway system or **metro** could not be simpler. Maps of the metro show that there are three lines – Line 1 coloured red, Line 2 coloured green and Line 3 coloured yellow (plus the Passante high-speed link, coloured blue). Cheap tickets can be bought from newsstands and tobacconists and are valid for 75 minutes anywhere on the system. Trains are generally clean and safe and you can reach 90 per cent of the places mentioned in this chapter by using the metro.

Museo Bagatti Valsecchi *

(Metro 3, Montenapoleone)

At via Santo Spirito 10, in the former house of the two Bagatti Valsecchi brothers, the collection gives a good indication of the tastes in art and furniture in the late 19th century. Rooms are devoted to tapestries, ivory work and paintings, along with a superb collection of furniture that children would have used in the 15th to 17th centuries. Open 10:00–18:00; closed on Monday.

Museo del Risorgimento *

Set in the Palazzo Moriggia, via Borgonuovo 23, the museum covers the course of the unification movement from the 1700s to 1870. Open 09:00–18:00; closed on Monday.

MORE CHURCHES

There are a vast number of historic churches in central Milan – enough to keep an enthusiast busy for a week. Some have already been mentioned. The following are all well worth a visit:

Basilica of San Lorenzo Maggiore **

(Metro 3, Missori)

The basilica, sometimes called 'alle Colonne', is located just to the south of the city centre near the old Porta Ticinese gateway. In front of the church are 16 Corinthian columns dating from the 2nd or 3rd century, originally belonging to an unidentified temple. San Lorenzo is Milan's oldest church, dating back to the 4th century, and its design is unlike any work of the Lombard architects. It suffered from many fires during the Middle Ages and had to be rebuilt after 1573 when the dome, the largest in Milan, collapsed. Don't miss the 5th-century Cappella di Sant'Aquilino, with its superb mosaics and the imposing statue of Emperor Constantine that marks the church's Roman connections.

Sant'Ambrogio ***

(Metro 2, Sant'Ambrogio)

Milan's best-known church can be found at the end of

THE AMATEUR BISHOP

Ambrose (Ambrogio) was a Roman governor sent to Milan in 374 to oversee the election of a new bishop. This was at a time of some theological turmoil, following the Arian controversy. Ambrose made an eloquent speech calming the crowds, who suddenly took up the chant 'Ambrose Bishop'. Although he had not even been baptized, he converted to Christianity immediately and in just over a week he had been made Bishop of Milan. He proved to be extremely successful at preserving the unity of the Church and establishing good relations between the Church and the Empire. Such was the reputation of this amateur bishop that he became the patron saint of Milan, and people from the city are still known today as *Ambrosiani*.

FIERA DI MILANO

Trade fairs have been held in Milan since 1920. In the early years it was a temporary affair on the parade ground of the Castello Sforzesca, but in 1985 a permanent exhibition centre was set up. Today, it hosts over 70 specialist shows a year, attracting 5 million visitors and 10,000 firms. New hotels have clustered around the Fiera, but during trade-fair weeks, most of the decent hotels in the city will be full.

Via San Vittore next to the 12th-century gate, the **Pusterla di Sant'Ambrogio**. The building is dedicated to St Ambrose, the city's patron saint, who founded the church in 379. It has been enlarged and rebuilt many times, but what we see today dates mainly from the 1080s. Sant'Ambrogio is widely considered to be the finest example of Romansque architecture in northern Italy and its pure architecture has been retained, with the round arches found throughout the complex of buildings. The interior of the basilica is basically severe, with the red-brick vaulting setting off the white walls. An exception to this austerity is the golden altarpiece or *paliotto*, a 9th-century masterpiece by Volvinio, composed of four silver and gold panels encrusted with pearls and precious stones. Notice, too, the 11th-century pulpit that is placed above a Romano Christian sarcophagus. The remains of St Ambrose are to be found in the crypt, along with those of Saints Gervasio and Protasio. The upper section of the portico (designed by Bramante) contains the **Museo della Basilica di Sant'Ambrogio**, which displays vestments, manuscripts, frescoes and even what is claimed to be the saint's bed. The museum is open 10:00–12:00 Monday, Wednesday–Friday; 15:00–17:00 Saturday and Sunday; closed on Tuesday. Next to Sant'Ambrogio is the **Catholic University of the Sacred Heart** located in the former Benedictine monastery. The university was founded in 1921 and the building retains two of Bramante's cloisters.

Below: *One of the many towers in the Romanesque Sant'Ambrogio complex.*

San Satiro **

(Metro 1, 3, Duomo)

Tucked in between tall buildings along the Via Torino is the little Renaissance gem of San Satiro. It was built largely by Donato Bramante in 1478 on the site of a 9th-century church. Bramante found that space was tight, so he built an exceptionally large nave and then relied on perspective and

optical illusions to achieve
effect. He created the illu-
sion of an apse by using
trompe l'oeil decoration.
Other features to note are
the octagonal baptistry
and the newly restored
Cappella della Pietà.
Outside, the brick-built
9th-century campanile is
the oldest in Lombardy.

Above: *Milan's taxis are always white in colour. They can only be boarded at official taxi ranks.*

Sant'Eustorgio *

(Metro 2, Stazione Genova)

Some way south of the historic centre and close to the *navigli* (canals), Sant'Eustorgio was built in the 11th century to house the relics of the Magi, which were taken to Milan by Bishop Eustorgius. In 1162, Frederick Barbarossa destroyed the building and took the relics to Cologne (they were not returned until 1903). The church was rebuilt in 1190, with the addition of a bell tower topped with a cone-shaped cusp. This is Milan's tallest bell tower and the first to have a clock. The simple façade gives little indication of the delights of the interior, which has so many art treasures it is almost like a museum. Not to be missed is the Portinari Chapel, which was originally commissioned by a Milanese banker. In the entrance is the magnificently carved raised tomb of St Peter the Martyr, built by Giovanni di Balduccio and dating from the mid-14th century. The other joy of the chapel is in the frescoes by Vincenzo Foppa that adorn the walls and ceiling. They were not discovered until 1878 when building work was taking place. Most of the artworks can be seen in the string of chapels of varying ages on the south side of the church.

San Maurizio *

(Metro 1, 2, Cadorna)

This church, in Corso Magenta, was begun in 1503 for a closed order of Benedictine nuns, and the design had

---

MILAN'S OUTDOOR MARKETS

Visiting one of Milan's street markets provides a wonderful insight into city life. There is plenty of choice. There are two **antique markets**, one along the Naviglio Grande on the last Sunday of the month and another in the Brera district in Via Fiori Chiari on the third Saturday of every month. **Flea markets** can be enjoyed in Via Lorenzini on Sunday mornings and in Viale Dannunzio all day on Sundays. Something special is the massive **clothes market** on Saturdays in Viale Papiniano. Remember that many of the markets may not operate during the month of August.

Above: *Stazione Centrale, Milan's main railway station, has an impressive façade built in the time of Mussolini.*

strict divisions between the public and the nuns. The exterior of the church is of little interest, but the interior has some superb frescoes attributed to Leonardo da Vinci's follower Bernardino Luini. They have been dated at around 1530 and are probably the artist's last work. In one of the chapels Luini has painted scenes from the life of St Catherine, including the *Decapitation of St Catherine*. It is believed that the face of the saint is actually a portrait of Countess Bianca Maria di Challant, who was actually beheaded herself in the courtyard of the Castello Sforzesco in 1516.

FURTHER OUT

A number of places in Milan that are well worth a visit are some way from the city centre and will require transport to reach them.

Stazione Centrale *
(Metro 2, 3, Centrale)
The Central Station was completed in 1931. It defies architectural definition and is really a political and ideological statement, reflecting Mussolini's obsession with making the trains run on time. Faced with light grey Aurisina stone, the façade alone is 207m (679ft) wide, and the roof is topped with winged horses. Inside the station there is a flight of steps leading to a concourse with a booking office, shops and a tourist information office. The platforms are spanned by massive glass and steel vaulting.

Pirelli Building *
(Metro 2, 3, Centrale)
Opposite the station is the elegant Pirelli Building. Built in the 1960s, it was Milan's first skyscraper and was built as the head office of the Pirelli organization. It is 124m (400ft) high and today acts as the headquarters of the Lombardy Regional Government.

Cimitero Monumentale
This cemetery has, somewhat bizarrely, become a tourist attraction. It is the burial ground of the great and good of

SORTING OUT YOUR TRAINS

The Italian State Railways (*Ferrovie dellos Stato*) provide an excellent service with fares at bargains rates. There are many types of train and their varying speeds will affect journey times. *EuroCity* are international express trains, while *InterCity* trains provide a luxury service between Italian cities. *Expressos* are long-distance trains, which, despite their name, can be slow because they stop at many stations. The slowest trains are the *diretto* and the *locale*.

Milan, each trying to outdo the other with the magnificence of their funerary monuments, hiring the best available sculptors for the task (*see* panel, this page).

San Siro Stadium *
(Metro 1, Lotto)

This stadium, at via Piccolomini 5, is now officially known as the Meazza, after a highly regarded footballer who played for both of Milan's teams – Inter and AC. Originally built in 1926, the stadium was modernized in the 1950s and again in 1990 when a roof was added. It now has a ground capacity of 85,000. Guided tours of the stadium take place daily from Monday–Saturday, except on days when matches are held. Also in the complex are a horse-racing track and a trotting stadium.

The Navigli **

To the southwest of the city centre are the remains of the once extensive canal system. First constructed in the 12th century, the canals linked Milan with the network of north Italian waterways. The canals brought Canoglia marble to the city to build the Duomo, along with fruit and vegetables from the countryside plus coal and salt from the ports. In the opposite direction went handmade goods such as textiles. Many of the canals were filled in during the 1930s, but it is interesting to note that Milan was Italy's 10th largest port as late as the 1950s. The area around the canals was once a staunch working-class area and it is still possible to see the old wash houses, the *Vicolo dei Lavandai*, that lined the canals. Today, however, the area has been gentrified. Real estate values have jumped and the old blocks of flats now command high prices, while boutiques and antique shops line the waterfront. The Navigli area also claims to have the trendiest restaurants in Milan. There is a popular antique market on the canal side on the last Sunday of the month during the summer, and a flea market each Saturday.

> **CIMITERO MONUMENTALE**
>
> It is hard to think of a cemetery as a tourist attraction, but Milan's *Cimitero Monumentale* is just that. The monuments to Milan's great and good include a pyramid, a life-size crucifiction and a sculpted recreation of the *Last Supper*. In the centre of the cemetery is a huge neo-Gothic temple, containing the tomb of writer Alessandro Manzoni and busts of Verdi and unification figures Cavour and Garibaldi. The *cimitero* is a long way from a metro station, so you will need a taxi to get there, but don't miss it.

Below: *The Pirelli Building, one of Milan's few skyscrapers, is a symbol of the city's postwar reconstruction.*

Milan at a Glance

BEST TIMES TO VISIT

Climatically, it is best to avoid Milan in winter when a raw fog can settle over the city for days on end, while August can be very hot and humid and many places close down for this period. **Spring**, early **summer** and **September** are the most comfortable times for visiting. Opera fans will need to come to the city in winter as the La Scala season begins in December.

GETTING THERE

Visitors arriving by **train** will find themselves at the Stazione Centrale, from where there are connections by metro, bus and taxi to other parts of the city. **Air** travellers will land at either **Linate Airport**, a few kilometres northeast of the city, or, more likely, at **Malpensa Airport**, 50km (30 miles) northwest of the city. Shuttle buses run regularly from both airports to Stazione Centrale. Visitors arriving by car will use the *autostrada*, but be warned that traffic levels in the city are high and a car is a dubious advantage. It is advisable to use the ATM parking areas on the outskirts of the city and then use public transport.

GETTING AROUND

Milan's **taxis** are white in colour, cheap and widely used by the business community. They cannot be hailed,

however, and must be picked up at authorized taxi ranks. Check that the meter is on. For a radio taxi ring 02 8585 or 02 6767. **Scooters**, **mopeds** and **cycles** are a good way of getting around if you are confident in the aggressive traffic. Cyclists should beware of the tramlines. The **public transport system** in Milan, involving buses, trams, trolley buses and the metro, is cheap and efficient, although often crowded. Trams and buses are yellow in colour. Tickets must be bought before boarding – available at newsstands and tabacconists. The **metro** has three lines – no. 1 is shown on maps in red, no. 2 is green and no. 3 is yellow. In addition there is the short Passante line, which is a fast rail link and shown on some maps in blue. Metro tickets are only valid for 75 minutes. Tourist tickets are good value and there are also weekly and monthly passes.

WHERE TO STAY

As Milan tends to cater for business travellers rather than tourists, its accommodation is largely of the expense account type and prices are notoriously high. There is little acceptable accommodation in the budget range, which tends to cater for newly arrived immigrants to the city and cannot really be recommended. Hotels cluster around the Central

Station and the Piazza della Repubblica, or near Fiera di Milano, the trade fair centre. Book in advance, as rooms tend to be snapped up, particularly during trade fairs and fashion weeks. The tourist offices provide a free hotel reservation service.

LUXURY

Four Seasons, via Gesù 8, tel: 02 77088, fax: 02 7708 5000. Generally reckoned to be the best hotel in town, with prices and service to match. Set in a converted monastery in the middle of the fashion district.
Grand Hotel et de Milan, via Manzoni 29, tel: 02 723 141, fax: 02 8646 0861. Historic hotel with Art Nouveau public rooms and antiques in bedrooms. Commendable restaurant.
Principe di Savoia, piazza della Repubblica 17, tel: 02 62301, fax: 02 653 799. Lavish hotel with garage and rooftop pool. Elegant rooms and own airport shuttle.

MID-RANGE

Manin, via Manin 7, tel: 02 659 6511, fax: 02 655 2160. Quiet location opposite Giardini Pubblici. Friendly service.
Una Hotel Scandinavia, via Fauché 15, tel: 02 336 391; fax: 02 3310 4510. New hotel close to the trade fair centre, good restaurant.
Madisson, via Gasparetto 8, tel: 02 6707 4150, fax:

Milan at a Glance

02 6707 5059. Friendly hotel in a quiet side street a short walk from the Stazione Centrale. Bed and breakfast only.

BUDGET
Youth Hostel
Milan's Youth Hostel, **Piero Rotta**, is located at Viale Salmoiraghi, tel: 02 3926 7095. Large modern building in the suburbs near the San Siro Stadium. Open 07:00–09:00 and 15:30–23:00. There is a 00:30 curfew! It is not possible to reserve ahead, so arrive early.

Camping
There are two camp sites close to the city:
Città di Milano, via G. Airaghi 61, tel: 02 4820 0134. Take the metro 1 to De Angeli and then bus 72.
Autodromo, Parco di Monza, tel: 02 3938 7771. Located in a park near the motor racing circuit, this camp site is only open in the summer months.

Milan offers just about every kind of food you care to think about, such as local cuisine, food from other regions of Italy, bland international dishes and food from other countries including Chinese, Indian, Japanese and South American. One thing is certain: it will be more expensive than anywhere else in Italy, but still reasonable by London or New York standards.

LUXURY
Savini, Galleria Vittorio Emanuele II, tel: 02 7200 3433. Has been serving classic Milanese delicacies since 1867; remains one of the top restaurants in the city.
La Scaletta, piazza Statione Porta Genova 3, tel: 02 5810 0290. Fresh ingredients in creative recipes. One of the best restaurants in Milan.
Aimo e Nadia, via Montecuccoli 6, tel: 02 416 886. Family restaurant; consistently high standards.

MID-RANGE
Trattoria Toscana Il Cerchio, via Galvani 15, tel: 02 670 0738. Popular and homely trattoria close to the Stazione Centrale.
Ponte Rosso, ripa di Porta Ticinese 23, tel: 02 837 3132. Excellent food in this friendly family establishment alongside the Naviglio Grande.
I Malavoglia, via Lecco 4, tel: 02 2953 1387. Good Sicilian food in a friendly atmosphere. Closed Monday.

BUDGET
There are any number of American fast-food outlets in Milan, where it is possible to eat cheaply. Pizzerias are also inexpensive, while many trattorias can be equally suitable for the budget-conscious. *Tavola Calda* (hot tables), where meals are taken standing up at the counter, are also affordable options.

Shopping in Milan can be a very enjoyable activity – providing you have a deep pocket. Most shopoholics head for the Quadrilatero d'Oro, the fashion centre of Milan, but shops throughout the city tend to be stylish, and window shopping can be almost as gratifying as actually buying. **Department stores** are not a common feature in Italy, but Milan has three – the classy La Rinascente whose restaurant has a superb view of the pinnacles of the Duomo; Coin on the Piazza Cinque Giornate; and Upim in Piazza San Babila. Milan also has a number of lively **street markets**, selling everything from antiques to the clothes worn by fashion models.

Tourist Information Centres: Tourist information is provided by the **Azienda di Promozione Turistica (APT)**. They have information about the city including free maps, hotel lists and information on cultural events. They are usually willing to book hotel reservations ahead. The main APT office is at via Marconi 1, at the side of the Duomo. Open 08:30–20:00 Mon–Fri, 09:00–13:00 and 14:00–19:00 Sat, 09:00–13:00 and 14:00–17:00 Sun; tel: 02 7252 4301, fax: 02 7252 4350.

3
Excursions from Milan

Milan is a handy centre for visiting a number of ancient cities and abbeys on the Plain of Lombardy. In many cases these towns flourished during the Dark Ages or the Middle Ages, but since then they have been left behind by Milan's determined growth. Fortunately this has meant that the towns have retained their old cobbled streets, ancient buildings and medieval atmosphere. **Bergamo**, for example, has a superb Old Town set up on a hill and protected by fortifications. **Pavia**, to the south of Milan, has retained its old Roman street plan and has an imposing Visconti castle and an ancient university. **Cremona**, away to the east, has a magnificent cathedral. It was the birthplace of Monteverdi and is noted for its manufacture of violins. The longest of the trips is to **Mantua**. Surrounded by lakes and swamps, the city is famous for its atmospheric squares. It was ruled by the wealthy Gorzaga family for centuries and they encouraged artists such as Andreas Montegna to base themselves in Mantua under their patronage. There are also two fine abbeys to visit. One, the **Abbey of Chiaraville**, is within Milan's city boundaries. The other, the **Certosa di Pavia**, just north of Pavia, is an ebullient mixture of Gothic and Renaissance styles. After Milan's Duomo, it is the most important monument in the region.

Fortunately, all the places mentioned above can easily be reached from Milan using public transport such as bus or train, although the use of a car would definitely be more convenient.

Don't Miss

*** Certosa di Pavia: Visconti Charterhouse – Lombardy's top monument after Milan's Duomo.
*** The Città Alta, Bergamo: the Venetian Empire's fortified hill town.
*** The Palazzo Ducale, Mantua: the stronghold and palace of the Gonzaga family.
** The Palazzo Tè: Federico Gonzaga's country retreat.
** The Basilica di San Michele Maggiore: the best of many Romansque churches.
** Monza's Duomo: beautiful cathedral containing the Iron Crown of Italy.

Opposite: *Bergamo – one of many ancient cities within easy reach of Milan.*

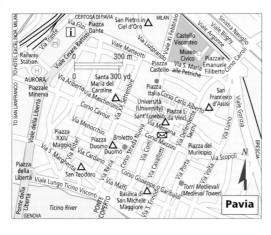

Chiaraville Abbey ★★

Once surrounded by water meadows, the abbey and its grounds have been swallowed up by the suburbs of Milan, but this does not detract from this impressive complex. The abbey was founded by French Cistercian monks in the mid-12th century. The bell tower was added in 1349 and it has a small church on either side. The huge main tower, which also dates from 1349, is a landmark for miles around. It has a range of double, triple and quadruple lancet windows and a vast number of small marble columns. Also worth seeing are the superb frescoes, the choir stalls and the rebuilt cloisters. Napoleon closed the monastery down in 1798 and it fell into disrepair. In recent years, however, the abbey has been restored and given back to the monks. The Abbey of Chiaraville can be reached by the number 13 tram from the Duomo, or from the nearest metro station, Corvetto, on line 3. It is open 09:00–12:00 and 14:00–17:00; closed on Monday.

MONZA

This small town of around 120,000 people is probably best known for its Grand Prix motor-racing circuit, but there is much more to see, including an impressive cathedral, the Duomo.

Located some 15km (9 miles) to the northeast of Milan, Monza was the place where the Lombard kings were crowned. The dominating building in the town is the **Duomo**, which dates from the 13th century, having been built on the site of a church that was set up by the Lombard Queen Theodolinda. A small remnant of this ancient church, depicting the queen and her family, can be seen above the main door of the cathedral. The façade,

---

THE GRAND PRIX AT MONZA

The Grand Prix motor-racing season lasts for almost the whole of the year. In Italy, the Grand Prix (*Grand Premio*) is held in mid-September in the Villa Reale Park at Monza, just to the northeast of Milan. By this time of year the Monza race is often crucial to the outcome of the championship. The Italian Ferraris in their traditional red colours lap at around 215kph (135mph) and receive huge support from the local fans. If you are not a motor-racing fan, stay away from the area on the day of the race, as the nearby roads have horrendous traffic jams. If you are a fan and want a ticket, contact the *Autodromo Nazionale di Monza*, tel: 039 248 212.

composed of green and white marble with a stunning rose window, is linked to a brick campanile dating from 1609. There is much to appreciate in the interior of the Duomo. Look for Theodolinda's Chapel to the left of the High Altar. As well as containing the queen's tomb, the chapel has some superb frescoes. The Duomo's most cherished relic is the **Iron Crown of Italy**, used to crown numerous Lombard kings, holy Roman emperors and, more recently, Napoleon. The jewel-encrusted gold crown has a rim of iron, said to have been made from one of the nails of the Cross. The cathedral museum is also worth visiting. One of its exhibits is Theodolinda's processional cross, given to her by Gregory the Great.

Parco di Monza *

Monza's other main attraction is the **Parco di Monza**, on the north side of the town. The park covers some 800ha (1976 acres), of which about 15 per cent is taken up with the motor-racing track and grandstands. In the middle of the park is Archduke Ferdinand of Austria's **Villa Reale**, built between 1776 and 1780 by Giuseppe Piermarini. The landscape around it is very much on English lines, with scattered trees, lakes and even a grotto. In 1805, Napoleon's viceroy in Italy expropriated the park, and handed it over to the people. Today, there are several sports available in the park, including golf, tennis, polo and swimming. Bicycles can be hired and there is a jogging track. Monza can be reached in 20 minutes by bus from Milan's Stazione Centrale.

PAVIA

The small town of Pavia is some 35km (22 miles) south of Milan and although it is rather somnolent today, this has not always been the case. Having been occupied by the Romans and the Goths, it became the capital of the Lombard Empire until it was finally eclipsed by Milan in the 11th century. Both Charlemagne and Barbarossa were crowned in Pavia, while one of its most famous denizens was Lanfranc, who became the first Archbishop of Canterbury after the Norman Conquest. Under the

> **THE IRON CROWN OF ITALY**
>
> The museum in the Duomo at Monza contains the Iron Crown of Italy. The 'iron' is in fact claimed to be the 'true nail' used to attach Jesus to the cross. It came to Monza via Queen Helena, who gave it to her son the Emperor Constantine. He had the nail beaten out into a strip that formed the rim of his jewel-encrusted crown. Over the centuries, more than 40 kings and holy Roman emperors have used the crown at their coronations. One of the most recent was Napoleon, who used the iron crown at his coronation in Milan Cathedral in 1805.

Below: *Italian restaurants use a variety of methods to attract diners.*

CLIMATE

Winter on the Plain of Lombardy is notoriously chilly and damp, with January temperatures averaging 1.1° C (34° F). **Summers** are hot and humid, with July temperatures at a mean of 24.8° C (76° F). **Precipitation** is generally light, coming mainly in the form of late summer thunderstorms. Some small amounts of **snow** can be expected in most winters.

Viscontis, Pavia became an intellectual centre and it was during this era that the university (probably the oldest in Italy) was founded.

The Duomo **

Head for the historic centre, which is partly pedestrianized and still retains its old Roman street plan. Dominating the core of the town is the rather stolid looking Duomo in Lombard Renaissance style. Work began on the cathedral in 1488 and Bramante, Leonardo, Amadeo and many others had a hand in its design. Its huge 19th-century dome, the third largest in Italy, towers above the rooftops. It was once accompanied by the Torre Civica, but this collapsed in 1989, killing four people.

The Basilica di San Michele Maggiore ***

Far more attractive than the Duomo is the Basilica di San Michele Maggiore, a fine Romanesque church dating back to 661. A major reconstruction took place in the 12th century after damage from a lightning strike. Some decorative sculpture can be seen, both on the frieze on the sandstone façade and on the capitals of the main columns in the interior. Also look for the Romanesque mosaic in the presbytery.

Below: *Pavia University has much of architectural interest, including a cloistered courtyard.*

There are a number of other churches of interest in Pavia, including the 12th-century **San Teodoro**, the 13th-century **San Francesco d'Assisi**, the Romanesque **San Pietro in Ciel d'Oro** with its gold ceiling, **Santa Maria del Carmine** dating back to 1390, and **San Lanfranco** with a memorial to the Archbishop of Canterbury.

The Ponte Coperto *

The River Ticino in Pavia is straddled by an attractive covered bridge, the **Ponte Coperto**. The original medieval covered bridge was just to the east, but was destroyed during World War II.

Castello Visconteo *

On the opposite side of the town is the **Castello Visconteo**. Built in 1360, it was partially destroyed in the Battle of Pavia in 1525. Three sides of the castle

survive and they now house the **Museo Civico**, which contains an excellent archaeological section. The art gallery has some important works by Italian and Dutch painters. The museum is open 10:00–12:00 and 14:30–16:00 Tuesday–Sunday, closed on Monday.

Above: *The Ponte Coperto or Covered Bridge spans the River Ticino in Pavia.*

The University *

Much of the northeastern part of the historic core of Pavia is taken up by the University. Within its campus are three of the remaining medieval towers for which the town was once famous, plus the crypt of the demolished 12th-century Church of Sant'Eusebio.

The Certosa di Pavia ***

The Certosa or Charterhouse is located 10km (6 miles) north of Pavia on the road to Milan. It can be reached by bus or train from Milan. It was built by Gian Galeazzo Visconti in the 1390s as a family mausoleum. Many of the architects and masons working on Milan's cathedral also spent time on the Certosa, but the main input was from Giovanni Antonio Amadeo, who was responsible for the design of the façade. The building shows a transition in styles from the Gothic to the Renaissance and is considered to be the most important monument in Lombardy after Milan's Duomo. The Certosa became a Carthusian monastery, but this was suppressed by Napoleon. In 1968 a group of Cistercian monks took over the monastery and maintain the old traditions, including

> **THE LATE LAMENTED MILLE MIGLIA**
>
> Although Grand Prix motor racing is alive and well, one popular race that has fallen by the wayside is the **Mille Miglia**. It was a race for sports cars over one lap of 1000 miles over public roads. It started from Brescia to the north of Milan and went along the Adriatic coast to Rome and back through the Apennines. In 1955 it was won by an Englishman, Stirling Moss, at an average speed of 158.5kph (98.5mph). Two years later, perhaps not surprisingly, the race was discontinued as it was considered too dangerous.

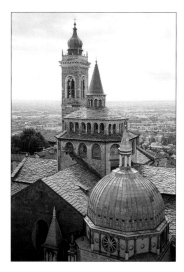

Above: *The view over the roofs of Bergamo from the Torre Civica.*

RED AND YELLOW HOUSES

Along the roads of northern Italy it is possible to see at regular intervals brightly painted red houses or **Casa di Cantonieri**. When Mussolini was intent on modernizing the Italian road system he provided a number of these red houses for families to live in free in return for maintaining the nearby stretch of road. He also provided a small number of yellow houses with big plots of land for very large families. As well as maintaining the roads, the yellow-housed families could grow fruit and vegetables in the gardens and sell the produce at local markets.

---

a vow of silence. A few of the monks are released from this vow in order to take guided tours around the Certosa. A highlight of the tour is the stunning façade of the church, which has more than 70 statues of saints and prophets. The interior has some impressive groin vaulting, a massive metalwork screen, marble mosaics on the floors, and beautiful stained-glass windows. The north transept contains the tomb of Ludovici el Moro and his wife Beatrice d'Este – brilliant work by Cristoforo Solari – while the south transept has the tomb of Gian Galeazzo Visconti. The tour leaves the south transept and enters the Little Cloister, with its terracotta decorations. From here there is a good view of the church's octagonal tower and cupola. This leads to the arcaded Great Cloister, with 122 arches supported by marble columns. The cloister is surrounded by the monks' comfortable cells – each has its own bedroom, study, chapel and walled garden. The tour ends in the refectory, which has ceiling frescoes by Bergognone and an elaborately carved pulpit, from where prayers are read to the silent diners. The Certosa is open 09:00–11:30 and 14:30–17:30 Tuesday–Sunday, although closing times may vary between summer and winter.

BERGAMO

Lying some 51km (31 miles) northeast of Milan, Bergamo can easily be reached by train, or by car using the Autostrada Serenissima, although parking can be very difficult. Bergamo was an independent city-state or *comune* during the 12th century, but after 1329 it came under Visconti control. Then, for the next 350 years, it was an outpost of the Venetian Empire – which explains the large number of statues of Venetian lions to be seen around the city. Bergamo is divided into two parts – the hilltop settlement of **Città Alta**, ringed by Venetian defensive walls, and **Città Bassa**, which spreads across the plains below. Bergamo has a proud military history,

producing the famous Venetian *condottiere* Bartolomeo
Colleoni and raising the largest contingent of any city for
Garibaldi's Red Shirts.

Città Bassa

Life in the modern lower town centres around the main
square, Piazza Matteotti. Here we find tree-lined arcades
or *senterione* with their popular cafés, and the **Teatro
Donizetti**, named after the locally born opera composer.
In Lower Bergamo there is an excellent art gallery, the
Pinacoteca dell'Accademia Carrara. It is housed in an
old palace in Via San Tomaso and is one of the top
galleries in northern Italy. Works by Botticelli, Bellini
and Titian are complemented by international artists
such as Van Dyck and Brueghel. It is open 09:30–12:30
and 14:30–17:30 daily. Admission is free on Sundays.

Città Alta

The Viale Vittorio Emanuele II leads to the lower station
of the funicular railway that takes you up into the heart
of the Città Alta. From the upper station it is just a short
walk to the charming **Piazza Vecchia**, which is surrounded by a wonderful collection of medieval and
Renaissance buildings. In the centre of the square is a
low-slung fountain protected by rather badly eroded
Venetian lions. On Sunday mornings, tables are set up in
the square for chess competitions. Dominating the piazza
is the 12th-century **Torre
Civica**, some 52m (170ft)
high. Steps or the lift lead
to the belfry, affording
panoramic views over the
roofs of Bergamo and the
surrounding countryside.
The belfry has a 15th-
century clock, and a huge
bell still tolls 180 times at
22:00 for the nightly curfew. At the upper end of
the Piazza Vecchia is the

> ### CONDOTTIERI
> *Condottieri* were soldiers
> of fortune in the service of
> Italian states during the late
> Middle Ages. As mercenaries,
> they had an interest in pro-
> longing the conflict and were
> often a liability to their
> employers. One of the most
> famous *condottieri* was
> **Bartolomeo Colleoni**
> (1400–76), a native of
> Bergamo who fought for and
> against most of the ruling
> dynasties of his time. The
> rebus of this fighting man
> says it all – it was in the form
> of *coglioni* (testicles) and
> appears on his coat of arms.
> The **Colleoni Chapel** at
> Bergamo, which he had built
> for a personal mausoleum, is
> one of the most stunning
> pieces of architecture in
> northern Italy – a fitting
> memorial for an old soldier.

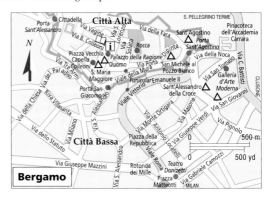

NORTHERN ITALIAN WINES

Some of the best wines in Italy are grown around the northern Italian lakes. When buying wine look for the letters DOC on the bottle. This stands for *Denominazione d'Origine Controllata* and means that only wines genuinely produced within a legally delimited area can be sold under the name of that area. Some of the better northern Italian wines include the popular white Soave and the cherry red Bardolino from the southeast shores of Lake Garda. The finest wines come from the Valtellina and the Franciacorta regions.

12th-century **Palazzo della Ragione**. A sloping covered stairway leads to the upper floor, which has a stone balcony and a Lion of St Mark in relief. The palace can only be visited when it is staging an exhibition.

The arches under the palace lead to the smaller, more intimate **Piazza Duomo**. Immediately ahead is the **Basilica of Santa Maria Maggiore**. Although much of the exterior of this church is hidden by other buildings, it is clear that it is one of the finest Romanesque churches in northern Italy. The delicate porch, built by Giovanni da Campione in 1360, is guarded by more Venetian lions. The interior is quite stunning, graced by some superb Flemish tapestries. Donizetti's tomb is tucked away against the west wall. Head for the presbytery where there are some wonderful examples of tarsias – inlaid woodwork – showing Old Testament scenes.

In comparison, the nearby 15th-century **Duomo** is something of an anticlimax, but worth looking around for its artworks. On the other side of the Basilica of Santa Maria Maggiore is another gem – the **Colleoni Chapel**. Dating from the 1470s, the chapel was designed by Amadeo for the tomb of the *condottiere* Bartolomeo Colleoni, and the sacristy of the basilica was knocked down to accommodate it. The incredibly ornate façade is built of polychromatic marbles and is a riot of lateral and rose windows, columns and balustrades leading up to the lantern-crowned dome. The interior of the chapel is equally impressive. On the top of Colleoni's tomb is an equestrian statue, while on another wall is the captain's daughter's tomb. Excellent paintings by Tiepolo line the dome. The chapel is open from 09:00–12:00 and 14:00–18:30 daily. It is closed on Monday.

Below: *A lion, symbol of the Venetian empire, guards the entrance to Bergamo's Basilica of Santa Maria Maggiore.*

The Città Alta also has several interesting churches, a Civic Archaeology Museum, a Natural History Museum with a life-sized reconstruction of a mammoth, a botanical garden, and two small museums devoted to Donizetti. If a picnic is the order of the day, then head for the **Rocca**. This is a ruined section of the old defensive fortifications, which has now been converted into shady gardens with fine views over the city and the surrounding plain.

Above: *The dome of Santa Maria Maggiore – Bergamo's finest church.*

CREMONA

The town of Cremona sits on the north bank of the River Po, to the southeast of Milan. It can be reached by train in around two hours. If you come by car, head for the Via Villa Glori car park, where you can exchange your vehicle for a bicycle for the day.

As with most of the towns of the Lombardy Plain, Cremona has had a chequered history. It was founded by the Romans but after the decline of their Empire it was repeatedly sacked by the Goths and Huns. Under the Lombards it became an independent *comune*. Later it came under the control of Milan's great dynasties, the Viscontis and the Sforzas, before becoming successively ruled by the Venetians, the Spanish and the Austrians. Among Cremona's famous sons are Virgil the Roman poet, Stradivarius the violin-maker and Claudio Monteverdi, one of the founders of opera as an art form.

Life in Cremona centres around the **Piazza del Comune**, which is dominated by the imposing 112m (370ft) **Torrazzo**. Built around 1250, it is reputedly the tallest bell tower in Italy. It is open 10:30–12:00 and 15:00–18:00 Tuesday–Sunday, April–October. From November–February it is open from 15:00–18:00 on Saturdays only. There are 502 steps to the top, but the

MASTER VIOLIN-MAKER

Although it was the Amati family of Cremona who made the first modern violins, it is the name of **Antonio Stradivarius** (1644–1737) that is always associated with the classic violin. During his career it is believed that Stradivarius made around 1200 violins, plus assorted mandolins, cellos and guitars. He used to scour the country looking for suitable woods such as poplar, maple and pear. It is said that every violin that he made was kept in his bedroom for a month so that his soul could be transferred to the instrument. The Stradivarius tradition is kept up in Cremona today, with around 60 workshops still producing violins.

climb is well worth the effort for the exceptional views. Alongside the tower, and linked to it by a portico, is the **Duomo**. The original church on the site was destroyed by an earthquake in 1117 and rebuilt by the Comacini masons, salvaging the original main door. The Duomo was originally a basilica, but when Gothic became the flavour of the day the two transepts were added. Recent restoration has revealed some primitive frescoes. Other features of interest include the Flemish tapestries, the twin pulpits, and the beautiful choir stalls inlaid with views of Cremona. Also in the Piazza del Comune are the **Battistero di San Giovanni** dating from 1167 and the **Loggia dei Militi** which has an outdoor pulpit used by the popular preachers of the time. Behind the loggia is the **Palazzo del Comune**. It dates from 1206 and is now the town hall.

Cremona is, of course, famous for its violins. The industry was started in the 16th century by the Amati family and followed on by Guarneri and Stradivarius. Today more than 50 violin-makers keep up the tradition. A comprehensive view of the subject can be enjoyed at the **Museo Stradivariano** in Via Pedestro, with more memorabilia at the **Museo Civico**, which also has a good section on archaeology. The School of Violin and Viola Makers also has a museum of stringed instruments at the **Palazzo dell'Arte**. Cremona has a clutch of fine churches, the best of which is 11th-century **Sant'Agata** in Corso Garibaldi, with some impressive frescoes.

MANTUA (MANTOVA)

Although it is a two-hour train journey from Milan, Mantau is well worth the effort of getting there. Its setting is unpromising – in the middle of a flat plain and almost completely surrounded by water where the River Mincio has swollen out into three lakes: Lago Superiore, Lago di Mezzo and Lago Inferiore. Influenced by the water, Mantua's climate can be raw and foggy in winter and hazy and humid in the summer.

Mantua had an uneventful history until it became an independent *comune* under the influence of the

---

HOME-GROWN FIREWATER

Those wishing to have a drink for effect rather than for taste will find that **grappa** fits the bill. This colourless spirit gains its name from the *graspa*, the detritus of the grapes after the wine has been fermented. These dregs are then distilled to make grappa. It is produced in **Bassano di Grappa**, halfway between Lake Garda and Venice, but is available all over northern Italy. Its acquired taste being such, it is probably not surprising that it was used as a medicine in the Middle Ages!

Gonzaga dynasty, which for three centuries ensured a peaceful way of life. The Gonzagas were enthusiastic sponsors of art and encouraged promising painters to take up residence in their court. The most important of these was Andrea Mantegna. After the Gonzagas' fall and the Austrian occupation, it was downhill all the way for Mantua, with the majority of the Gonzagas' art treasures scattered around the art galleries of Europe. Today, it has spawned some ugly Fascist-era suburbs and some nasty industrial estates on the outskirts, yet the centre of the town is virtually unspoiled, with four interconnecting cobbled squares and a host of restored palaces and churches, making this one of the gems of northern Italy.

Most of the monumental buildings are found in the northeast corner of the town. As you approach from the Lago di Mezzo, where cars can be parked, you reach the imposing **Castello di San Giorgio** guarding the entrance to the town. The castle was built between 1395 and 1400 during the time of Francesco I Gonzaga. Opposite the castle on the right-hand side of the road is the House of Rigoletto, with a statue of the court jester in the garden.

You now approach Mantua's largest square, the **Piazza Sordello**. Almost the whole of the southeast side of the square is taken up with the façade of the **Palazzo Ducale**, the home of the Gonzagas. The huge complex is almost like a city in itself, with streets, courtyards, gardens and over 500 rooms covering 34,000m^2 (366,860 sq ft). When

TOILETS
Public toilets are almost non-existent in Italy. Where they can be found, they may be in a less than hygienic condition. Do what the Italians do – slip into the nearest bar or even hotel foyer and use their facilities. This is standard practice and will not cause offence.

Below: *Mantua's main square, the busy Piazza Sordello.*

To Tip or Not to Tip?

It is always important to travellers to know whether or not tipping is expected. In Italy, a tip is always appreciated, but don't pay up unless the service is good. In restaurants, check the bill to see if service is included. If not, it is usual to add between five and ten per cent. In cafés and bars, a small tip will be sufficient. Porters in airports and hotels generally expect a small tip. On excursions, coach drivers and guides are normally rewarded if they have given good service. In the days of the lire the offer of coins was an insult. Today, euro coins are acceptable.

the building was ransacked in 1630, it is said that it took 80 carriages to take away the 2000 works of art. There are three main structures – the original **Corte Vecchia**, the 14th-century **Castello**, and the **Corte Nuovo**. Visits are by guided tour only and they take about 1½ hours. The highlights of the tour are the **Camera degli Sposi**, containing Mantegna's frescoes of the Gonzaga family, and the private **apartments of Isabella d'Este**, which include some miniature rooms, once thought to be for the dwarfs whom she collected to cheer her up! The Palazzo Ducale is open 08:45–19:15 Tuesday–Sunday; June–September until 23:00.

Opposite the Palazzo Ducale on the corner of Piazza Sordello is the **Duomo**. It was built in the 13th century and shows a mixture of styles. The rather dull façade is neoclassical, the side facing the square is Gothic, and other parts of the exterior, including the bell tower, have Romanesque elements. The interior is more interesting, having been rebuilt by Giulio Romano after a fire in 1545. It has a nave and four broad aisles divided by elegant fluted columns. On the other side of the square are the **Bonacolsi Palaces**, dating from pre-Gonzaga times. Rising from their crenellated roofs is the notorious **Torre della Gabbia**, said to contain an iron torture cage in which prisoners were suspended over the city.

An archway leads through to the **Piazza Broletto**, where we find the town hall containing the **Museo Tazio Nuvolari**, dedicated to a local hero who was a racing driver. Another portico marks the entrance to the charm-

Below: *The Rotonda di San Lorenzo, Mantau's oldest church.*

ing **Piazza dell'Erbe**, lined with arcaded cafés and stalls. Sunk slightly below the level of the square is Mantua's oldest church, the 11th-century **Rotonda di San Lorenzo**, said to be modelled on the Church of the Holy Sepulchre in Jerusalem. It has been sympathetically restored during recent years and it is possible to see some 12th- and 13th-century frescoes.

Dominating the nearby **Piazza Mantegna** is the **Basilica di Sant'Andrea**, designed by Alberti. The façade takes the form of a triumphal arch, while the interior is based on the traditional design of an Etruscan temple with a single barrel vaulted nave and numerous high-arched side chapels. The tomb of Andrea Mantegna

Above: *A wedding scene at the Basilica di Sant'Andrea in Mantua.*

is in the first chapel on the left. The dome, which was completed in 1782, rises to 80m (262ft). Under the dome is an octagonal balustrade, which is immediately above the crypt. This houses two sacred reliquaries said to contain the blood of Christ and given to St Andrew by Longinus, the Roman centurion who pierced Christ's side with a lance.

On the southern outskirts of Mantua is the summer residence of the Gonzagas, the **Palazzo Tè**. It was built by Federico Gonzaga as a retreat from the Palazzo Ducale where he could see his horses and his mistress, Isabella Boschetta, who was not approved of by Federico's mother. The word *tè*, incidentally, comes from *tejeto*, meaning drainage canal. The complex was designed by Giulio Romano and it is considered to be his greatest work. The main attraction for visitors is the series of rooms with extraordinary frescoes, trompe l'oeil and paintings, showing that Romano was given full permission to shock and amaze. Many of the classical frescoes are erotic, even vaguely pornographic, but never dull. The **Sala dei Cavalli** has portraits of the best horses from the Gonzaga stable; the **Sala di Psyche** has frescoes showing the wedding banquet of Cupid and Psyche; and in the **Sala dei Giganti** there is a remarkable fresco showing Jupiter's rage towards the Titans who had dared to climb Mount Olympus. The Palazzo Tè is open 09:00–18:00 Tuesday–Sunday; closed Monday.

A VARIETY OF PASTA

A pasta course is an essential part of an Italian meal, but the pasta itself and the sauces that go with it vary tremendously. There are said to be over 100 varieties of pasta, depending on its shape. It can, for example, be flat, tubular, straw-like, twirled, conch-like, rolled or filled. It can also vary in its ingredients, with flour, eggs, oil and salt forming the basics. The sauces to accompany the pasta change according to the region.

Excursions From Milan at a Glance

All the cities mentioned in this chapter are on the Plain of Lombardy, which is notorious for its days of raw fog in the winter and the heat and humidity in the summer. Choose spring and autumn for the most comfortable sightseeing weather. Local saints' days are always enjoyable times to visit, but accommodation may be hard to find on these occasions.

All the historic towns mentioned are within easy reach of Milan. A **car** can give flexibility and convenience, the efficient *autostrada* system allowing distances to be covered quickly. Visitors wishing to use public transport will find that all the towns are linked with Milan by **rail** and in many cases by **bus**.

All the towns described have compact historic cores, where most of the sites can easily be visited on foot. Indeed, in many cases cars may be banned. Otherwise, **taxis** are readily available.

Cheaper hotels tend to be booked up with immigrant workers and few can be recommended. Hotels close to Milan can be fully booked well in advance during trade fair weeks.

LUXURY

Hotel de la Ville, viale Regina Margherita 15, Monza, tel: 039 382 581, fax: 039 367 647. The town's top hotel with a view overlooking the park.

Moderno, viale Vittorio Emanuele II 45, Pavia, tel: 0382 303 401, fax: 0382 25225. Plush hotel close to the railway station.

Excelsior San Marco, piazza della Repubblica 6, Bergamo, tel: 035 366 111, fax: 035 366 175. One of the best hotels in town with air-conditioned rooms and a reputable restaurant.

Impero, piazza della Pace 21, Cremona, tel: 0372 460 337. An Art Deco palace provides a wonderful setting for this glamorous hotel.

San Lorenzo, piazza Concordia 14, Mantua, tel: 0376 220 500, fax: 0376 327 194. Delightful setting overlooking the Piazza dell' Erbe. Leisure facilities.

MID-RANGE

Excelsior, piazza Stazione 25, Pavia, tel: 0382 28596 fax: 0382 26030. Comfortable hotel in a handy location.

San Vigilio, via San Vigilio 15, Bergamo, tel/fax: 035 437 3004. Marvellous position near the top of the western funicular.

Duomo, via Gonfalonieri 13, Cremona, tel: 0372 35242. Comfortable hotel a short walk from the Piazza del Comune. Good restaurant.

ABC, piazza Don Leoni 25, Mantua, tel: 0376 323 347. Rooms round a courtyard. Close to station.

BUDGET

Aurora, viale Vittorio Emanuele II 25, Pavia, tel: 0382 23664, fax: 0382 21248. Has showers in all rooms. Close to station.

Astoria, via Bordigallo 19, Cremona, tel: 0372 461 616, fax: 0372 461 810. Popular, near the Piazza del Comune.

Peter Pan, citadella Piazza Giulia 3, tel: 0376 392 637. Mantua's only cheap hotel, a few minutes' walk across the lake.

Youth Hostel

The only youth hostel is in Bergamo:

Youth Hostel, via G. Ferraris 1, Bergamo, tel: 035 361 724. Out of town – take the no. 14 bus.

Camp Sites

There are three handily placed camp sites:

Ticino, via Mascherpa 10, Pavia, tel: 0382 527 094. Open April–November. No. 4 bus from the railway station.

Parco al Po, Via Longo Po Europa, Cremona, tel: 0372 21268, fax: 0372 27137. Open May–September. Take the no. 1 bus from the railway station.

Corte Chiara, Porto Mantovano outskirts, Mantua, tel: 0376 390 804. Open

Excursions From Milan at a Glance

May–September. Small site, booking essential.

WHERE TO EAT

Eating out in the historic cities of the Plain of Lombardy is generally cheaper than in Milan, but there is not the wide range of international cuisine. Local and regional specialities are the order of the day, such as the notorious Spezzatino di Mantua – donkey stew. Restaurants with outside tables in the main squares of the towns are likely to be more expensive than those in side streets.

LUXURY

Ceresole, via Ceresole 4, Cremona, tel: 0372 30990. High-class Cremonese cuisine.

L'Aquila Nigra, via Vicolo Bonacolsi 4, Mantua, tel: 0376 327 180. All Mantua's local specialities in a frescoed dining room near the Palazzo Ducale. Closed Mondays.

Da Vittorio, via Giovanni XXIII 21, Bergamo, tel: 035 218 060. One of Italy's top restaurants. Specializes in seafood. Closed Wednesday.

Hotel de la Ville's Derby Grill, viale Regina Margherita 15, Monza, tel: 039 382 581. Undoubtedly the best food in Monza.

Locanda Vecchia Pavia, via Cardinal Riboldi 2, Pavia, tel: 0382 304 132. Ancient restaurant next to the cathedral, serving local dishes in nouvelle cuisine style.

MID-RANGE

Vesuvio, piazza Libertà 10, Cremona, tel: 0372 434 858. Reasonably priced local food.

Pavesi, Piazza dell'Erbe, Mantua, tel: 0376 323 627. Friendly restaurant, one of several in the atmospheric little square. Local specialities. Closed on Thursdays.

Al Garibaldini, via S. Longino 7, Mantua, tel: 0376 328 263. Restaurant in a characterful house in the historic core. Closed on Wednesdays.

Taverna del Colleoni, Piazza Vecchia, Bergamo, tel: 035 232 596. Atmospheric restaurant in the old square, serving classical Italian food. Closed on Mondays.

Antica Osteria del Vino Buono, Piazza Mercato delle Scarpe, Bergamo, tel: 035 247 993. Friendly *osteria* next to the upper funicular station. Closed on Mondays.

Dell'Uva, piazza Carrobiolo 2, Monza, tel: 039 323 825. Reasonably priced regional food in the centre of town.

Antica Osteria del Previ, via Milazzo 65, Pavia, tel: 0382 26203. On the bank of the Ticino River. Noted for its frogs' legs, snails and river fish.

BUDGET

Head for pizzerias and small trattorias for budget food.

Fragoletta Antica Osteria, piazza Arche 5, Mantua, tel: 0376 323 300. Little ambience, but great cooking. Closed on Mondays.

Pizzeria Cremonese, piazza Roma 39, Cremona. Pizzas plus local dishes.

La Colombina, borgo Canale 12, Bergamo, tel: 035 261 402. Terrace restaurant serving local specialities. Closed on Mondays.

Piedigrotto, corso Libertà 15, Mantua, tel: 0376 327 014. Good traditional pizzas. Closed on Wednesdays.

USEFUL CONTACTS

There are **APT Tourist Information Offices** in the following towns:

Cremona: Piazza del Comune, opposite the Duomo. Open 09:00–12:00 and 15:00–18:00 Monday–Saturday, 09:45–12:00 Sunday, tel: 0372 23233, website: www.cremonaturismo.com Apart from maps and brochures, they have a list of violin-makers' workshops.

Mantua: piazza Mantegna 6, tel: 0376 328 253. They have a useful map of the town with information on the major sites.

Bergamo: viale Vittorio Emanuele II 20. Open 09:00–12:30 and 14:00–17:30 Monday–Friday, tel: 035 210 204, website: www.apt. bergamo.it Another office in Bergamo Alta is at vicolo Aquila Nera 2, off the Piazza Vecchia, and it is open all year round, tel: 035 232 226.

Pavia: via F. Filzi 2, tel: 0382 22156. Open 08:30–12:30 and 14:00–18:00 Monday–Saturday.

4
Lakes Maggiore, Orta and Varese

Lake Maggiore stretches for 64km (40 miles) from north to south, making it the second largest of the northern Italian lakes. The lake is fed by the **River Ticino** from the north and the **River Toce** from the northwest. It is drained in the south by the Ticino, which runs in a large arc to the west of Milan, before joining the Po at Pavia. The most northerly one-fifth of Lake Maggiore is in the Swiss Canton of Ticino, with the stylish **Locarno** its main town. The western shore of the lake is in Piedmont, but the eastern shore comes under the administration of Lombardy.

The Romans called Maggiore *Lacus Verbanus* after the verbena plant that grows prolifically around its shores. Maggiore had close links with dynastic families such as the **Viscontis** and the **Borromeos**. The latter still own large tracts of land and islands in the area. In the 19th century, Lake Maggiore was an important and enjoyable part of the **Grand Tour**, and writers, artists and musicians, such as Goethe, Byron and Toscanini, frequently visited the lake. Queen Victoria stayed at Baveno and English tourists have been coming to Lake Maggiore ever since.

The leading resort on the lake is **Stresa**, which overlooks the enchanting **Borromean Islands**, an essential excursion for all visitors. A road encircles the lake and it is possible to drive its 162km (100 miles) in a day, but most visitors would want to take longer to enjoy Lake Maggiore's charms. To the west of Maggiore is the smaller **Lake Orta**. Its main attraction is the town of **San Giulio** and the island of the same name. East of Maggiore are a clutch of smaller lakes, the largest of which is **Lake Varese**.

DON'T MISS

*** Borromean Islands: Isola Madre, Isola dei Pescatori and Isola Bella should be on everyone's itinerary.
*** Orta San Giulio and **Isola San Giulio:** the attractive village and romantic island are star attractions.
** Stresa: an important and well-situated resort.
** Statue of San Carlo Borromeo: enormous 23m (75ft) statue of one of Milan's best-known archbishops.
** Villa Taranto: early 20th-century gardens near Pallanza.
* Sacro Monte: 21 chapels with over 350 statues.

Opposite: *Lake Maggiore, with the Borromean Islands, viewed from Stresa.*

CLIMATE

The Lake Maggiore area has a less extreme climate than Milan and the Plain of Lombardy. **Winter** temperatures are tempered by the water of the lakes and frost is rare at lake levels, allowing subtropical plants to survive. Moderate snowfall is experienced on the nearby hills and this increases in the Alps. **Summers** are warm at lake level, averaging 24°C (75°F). **Rainfall** is light to moderate with late-summer thunderstorms common.

Below: *The waterfront at Locarno is backed by wooded hills.*

THE SWISS NORTH

The northern 20 per cent of Lake Maggiore is in Swiss territory, where the main town is **Locarno**. Once under the control of Milan, it fell into Swiss hands in 1512 and has remained there ever since. Locarno has a sheltered south-facing position and it has developed over the years as a health resort. The **Locarno International Film Festival** is held in the town every August. It also has a popular **casino** in Lago Zorsi 1. (Open 12:00–02:00 Sunday–Thursday; 12:00–04:00 Friday–Saturday.) The town is distinguished by pleasant public gardens, elegant squares and galleried shops. The 14th-century **Castello Visconti** was partially destroyed by the Swiss and its remains now house a small museum containing a strange mixture of archaeological artefacts and modern art. (Open 10:00–12:00 and 14:00–17:00 Tuesday–Sunday). It is also worth taking the cable car to the **Church of Madonna del Sasso**, which dates from 1480. Its altarpiece displays the *Flight Into Egypt*, by Bramantino. A chair lift then leads up to **Cimetta di Cardado** at a height of 1671m (5482ft), from where there are spectacular views along the lake.

Separated from Locarno by the reedy delta of the River Maggia is the small town of **Ascona**. Once a small fishing port, it is now growing as a resort and attracting a lively artistic community. Just offshore is a group of small islands known as the **Isoli di Brissago**, the largest of which has some subtropical gardens and a 16th-century church. The town of **Brissago**, after which the islands were named, is the last settlement before the Italian border is reached. Brissago is a minor health resort, but ironically the town is dominated by its huge tobacco factory.

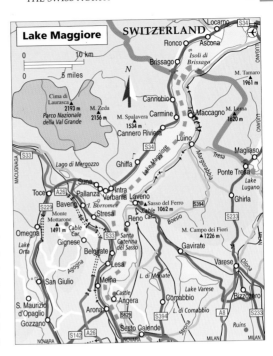

THE PIEDMONT SHORE OF LAKE MAGGIORE

The first settlement of any size on the Piedmont shore is the medieval town of **Cannobio**. With small squares, cobbled alleys and an attractive lake frontage, it is a pleasant place to stop for a few hours, particularly on a Sunday when there is a quayside market. The main place of historic interest in Cannobio is the **Santuario della Pietà**, a church built to house the miraculous picture of the dead Christ, which was once said to have shed real blood (*see* panel, page 71). A scenic excursion from Cannobio is up the valley behind the town, leading to a spectacular gorge and the little church of **Santa Ana**. The narrow mountain road eventually reaches the **Val Vigezzo**, the valley followed by the spectacular Domodossola–Locarno railway.

As the road approaches **Cannero Riviera**, a group of small, low rocky islands can be seen close to the shore.

FACTS ABOUT LAKE MAGGIORE

Length:
64km (40 miles).
Average width:
4.8km (3 miles).
Maximum depth:
372m (1220ft).
Water area:
215km² (84 sq miles).

Above: *The popular resort of Baveno, on the western arm of Lake Maggiore, was once favoured by Queen Victoria.*

Capped with ruined castles, they were once the haunt of a group of extremely bloodthirsty brigands, who were eventually dealt with by the Viscontis. Cannero is almost a mirror image of Cannobio, with cobbled streets, picturesque houses and an attractive little harbour. The next stop is **Ghiffa**, which once had an important hat-making industry, but the factory, once the largest in Italy, closed in 1981. You can, however, learn about the industry at the local **Hat Museum** (open 15:30–18:30 Saturday and Sunday throughout the year).

A minor conurbation has been formed at a fork in the lake. The towns of Intra, Pallanza and Suna were merged in 1939 to form **Verbania**. The most industrial of the three is Intra, which gets its name from its situation between two streams. A car ferry, the only one on Lake Maggiore, runs across to Laveno, the journey taking 20 minutes. (For information, tel: 03 233 1480.) Pallanza has an attractive lake frontage with parks and gardens, including a string of exuberant fountains, backed by restaurants and bars. It is worth visiting the **Church of San Leonardo**, which is close to the waterfront. This dates back to the 16th century and its 65m (213ft) bell tower is an imposing landmark. Back in the town, in Piazza Cavour is the **Museo del Paesaggio**, a museum of landscape painting set in an old palace. There are also some sculptures and some local archaeological finds. (Open 10:00–12:00 and 15:00–18:00 Tuesday–Sunday April–October.) Just offshore is the **Isolino di San Giovanni**, the fourth and smallest of the Borromean Islands and the only one that cannot be visited. It was a favourite hideaway of Arturo Toscanini, the conductor.

THE LOCARNO PACT OF 1925

The most important nations in Europe sent representatives to Locarno, on Lake Maggiore, in October 1925, in the interests of European peace. The agreement guaranteed the post-World War I European frontiers and was designed to prevent all future European wars. Unfortunately, 11 years later, in 1936, Adolf Hitler tore up the Treaty – and the rest, as they say, is history.

A major attraction at Verbania is the **Villa Taranto** (*see* panel, page 72). The villa itself is not open to the public, but is widely used for congresses and conferences – the EU prime ministers met there recently. The gardens are open daily from 08:30–19:30 or sunset, April–October.

Between Verbania and the Via Vigezzo is the **Parco Nazionale della Val Grande**, a true wilderness and the least inhabited area of the Alps. Although the park only rises to just over 2000m (6500ft) there are spectacular views of the Alps to the north. There are barren peaks, steep-sided gorges, bubbling streams and forests at lower levels, along with a vast array of Alpine flowers. This is good hiking country for the experienced mountain enthusiast, but there are few trails and only a small number of spartan huts.

A small arm of Lake Maggiore leads northwest to meet the road from the Simplon Pass. The road runs close to the small reed-fringed **Lago di Mergozzo**, once part of the main lake but cut off by silt deposits from the river. The lakeside road now swings back southeastwards towards the resort of **Baveno**, made popular by Queen Victoria, who stayed here at the Villa Clara (now known as the Castello Branca). The town is backed by a

THE SANTUARIO DELLA PIETÀ

Back in 1522 a picture of the dead Christ being taken down from the cross was hanging in a house in Cannobio when a strange thing occurred – Christ's wounds in the picture began to bleed. Shortly afterwards Cannobio was spared when all the towns around were decimated by the plague. San Carlo Borromeo decreed that this was a miracle and ordered that a church should be built to house the picture, which was put in an elaborate frame. It can be seen today in the Santuario della Pietà – although, oddly, there is no sign of any blood stains on the picture.

Left: *Stresa's hotels and restaurants are among the best in the Italian lake area.*

VILLA TARANTO

The villa was built in 1875, but by the turn of the century it had become derelict. Both the villa and the land were bought in 1931 by a Scots captain, Neil McEacharn. He spent the next 10 years creating the finest botanical gardens in northern Italy. Covering some 20ha (65 acres), they contain over 20,000 species of plants, including Amazonian lilies, maples, bottle brushes, monkey puzzles, handkerchief trees and many more. The gardens are particularly attractive in late spring, when the azaleas and rhododendrons are in full bloom. As McEacharn had no descendants, he left the gardens and villa to the Italian state.

huge pink cliff, marking the granite quarries that supplied the material for Milan's Galleria Vittorio Emanuele II and the Basilica of St Paul's in Rome. Graceful villas line the road and shoreline, while in the centre of the town the 11th-century church of **Santi Gervasio e Protasio** in the main square has a 12th-century façade and a Romanesque bell tower. It is worth seeking out Baveno's most photographed building, the **Casa Morandi**, with its highly original exterior stairways.

STRESA

Without doubt, Stresa is the most attractive town on Lake Maggiore, its popularity having increased considerably after the opening of the Simplon Tunnel in 1906. Its string of large and elegant hotels along the lake shore are widely used by tour parties and for conferences. Lush gardens and villas line the shore from where there are stunning views of the Borromean Islands. The old town centre focuses on the triangular **Piazza Cadorna**, with its pavement cafés and boutiques. From here cobbled alleyways lead in all directions. Among Stresa's attractions are the **Villa Pallavicino**, a botanical garden and animal park to the south of the town (open 09:00–18:00 from March–October), and **Villa Ducale**, with a small museum and connections with the Catholic philosopher, Antonio Rosmini. (Open daily 09:00–12:00 and 15:00–18:00.)

EXCURSIONS FROM STRESA

Just north of Stresa, a cable car climbs up to **Monte Mottarone**, 1491m (4891ft), from where there are superb views of the lake and away to Monte Rosa and other Alpine peaks. The cable car runs

Below: *Stresa's lake shore is graced by elegant hotels and attractive gardens.*

at half-hourly intervals, from 09:30–12:00 and again from 13:30–17:00, taking 18 minutes to reach the top station. From here, there are a number of hiking routes, and mountain bikes can be hired. It is also possible to drive up to Monte Mottarone via a toll road, passing en route the **Giardino Alpinia**. These Alpine rock gardens are a must for keen botanists. (Open from 09:00–18:00 Tuesday–Saturday, April–October; 09:00–18:30 Sundays and holidays.) Also en route, in the hamlet of Gignese, is quite an unusual **Umbrella Museum**, devoted to the history and making of umbrellas, once an important industry in these parts. (Open 10:00–12:00 and 15:00–18:00 Tuesday–Sunday, April–September.)

Above: *The Alpine village of Macugnaga is easily reached from Stresa.*

SAN CARLO BORROMEO (1538–84)

Charles Borromeo was undoubtedly the most influential and distinguished churchman of his day. He was a cardinal by the age of 22 and became Archbishop of Milan when he was 26 – a startling rise up the career ladder helped by a push from below by his uncle, Pope Pius IV. San Carlo did, however, fulfil a strong disciplinary role in the church, saving sacred church music and ending the somewhat comfortable life of the clergy. In doing so he made enemies, and survived an assassination attempt in Milan Cathedral. But he was a courageous man and risked his life comforting the victims of the plague. He was canonized in 1610 and his feast day is on 4 November.

Macugnaga **

A coach trip to Macugnaga, an Alpine village and ski resort, is a very popular excursion from Stresa. The route initially follows the Dossola River past the Candoglia marble quarries and then heads west into the Anzasca Valley through some spectacular scenery. Many more quarries are seen near Castiglione and these have supplied the marble steps for the United Nations building in New York. The valley becomes increasingly narrow and eventually the village of **Macugnaga** is reached. With its wooden chalets, Alpine cattle and the backdrop of the snowcapped peaks of **Monte Rosa**

reaching up to 4638m (14,136ft), this is a totally different world to Lake Maggiore. Macugnaga is a popular ski resort, and a cable car and chair lift lead up to the slopes above the tree line. The village itself has a pretty square with a tourist office and a number of restaurants and bars. The church is worth a visit. Although plain on the exterior, with a short copper spire, the interior is flamboyant and ornate, more in the Spanish style – which is perhaps not surprising as the Spaniards occupied the valley for 200 years.

Above: *Isola dei Pescatori is notable for its fine fish restaurants.*
Opposite: *Terraced gardens with statues and exotic plants form the eastern end of Isola Bella.*

The Hundred Valleys Line ★★

Another excursion from Stresa that will particularly appeal to the railway enthusiasts is the trip along the **Vigezzo Valley**. A train is taken to Domodossola, where a change is made to a light railway. This runs along the Vigezzo, a route known as the **Hundred Valleys** because of the vast number of tributaries that join the main valley. The line ends up at **Locarno**, where there is time for shopping before taking the lake steamer back to Stresa, making a magnificent day out.

THE BORROMEAN ISLANDS

The Borromeo family became the rulers of this part of northern Italy in the 15th century and still own much of the area today, including the four little islands that occupy the northwest arm of Lake Maggiore. **Isolino di San Giovanni** is privately owned and not accessible to visitors, but the other three islands form the major tourist attraction in the whole of the Italian lakes. All three are readily accessible by ferry and motor launch from Stresa, Baveno and Pallanza. A night trip around the islands when they are floodlit is a memorable experience.

THE PUPPET THEATRE

'Come children, let us shut up the box and the puppets, for our play is played out', said a character in Thackeray's *Vanity Fair*. Visitors can imagine the Borromeo children receiving such instructions when they see the charming puppet theatre sets in one of the rooms in the villa on Isola Madre. Beautifully made, with their porcelain faces and traditional clothes, the puppets and marionettes recall the days before the advent of mass media when entertainment was a family tradition.

Isola Madre

This is the largest island and the nearest to Pallanza. It is open to the public from mid-March to late September 09:00–17:30. There are superb informal gardens that are particularly attractive in late spring, with azaleas, rhododendrons and hydrangeas, plus a host of specimen trees, dominated by a huge 300-year-old weeping silver cupressus. There is a small aviary, and white peacocks and ornamental pheasants strut around at will. Guided tours are available around the 16th-century villa, which has a collection of paintings and is the home of the Borromeo family's puppet theatre (*see* panel, page 74). There is a small restaurant near the landing stage.

Isola dei Pescatori ***

This island was once a working fishing village and it is still possible to see the occasional fishing net hanging up to dry and a few of the distinctive fishing boats with their curved roofs and large lights. Most of the fishing now takes place at night in the quieter northern part of the lake. Take time to wander around the picturesque cobbled alleys and sample a fish lunch at one of the

---

ROCK AND STONE

The area to the northwest of Lake Maggiore is renowned for the quality of its building stones. Very noticeable from the lake is the pink cliff behind the town of **Baveno**. This is the granite quarry that supplied the stone for La Scala Opera House and the Galleria Vittorio Emanuele II in Milan. On the eastern side of the Dossola Valley are the **Baveno** marble quarries that supplied the material for Milan's Duomo. They are still open today but are only allowed to provide marble for repairs to the cathedral – and nowhere else. The **Anzasca Valley** has a whole string of quarries that supply fine marble all over the world, including that used for the steps of the United Nations building in New York.

A GIANT OF A MAN

Just outside the lakeside town of **Arona** is the enormous statue of **San Carlo Borromeo**. Commissioned by Federico, a nephew of San Carlo, it was designed by Cerano in 1614 and erected in 1624. Made of copper, the statue is 23.4m (77ft) in height and rests on a stone plinth 11.7m (38ft) high. The head has a circumference of 6.50m (21ft), the eyes are 0.5m (1.6ft) wide, the nose is 0.85m (2.8ft) long and the thumb is 1.4m (4.5ft) long – surely the greatest saint ever!

lakeside restaurants. The 11th-century (but much renovated) little church is also worth a visit, along with the immaculately kept adjacent cemetery.

Isola Bella

This is the nearest of the islands to Stresa and tends to be the most crowded. In the 17th century Carlo III Borromeo decided that he would convert what was a flat rocky island into a paradise for his wife Isabella. He commissioned the architect, Angelo Crivelli, to carry out the transformation. Tons of earth were brought from the mainland to create a garden of ten terraces in the formal Italian style, with fountains, grottoes and statues of gods and cherubs, complemented by exotic shrubs and trees. The gardens culminate at the eastern end of the island with a huge ornate terrace looking like the bridge of a liner – just a little 'over the top'. A sumptuous **palazzo** (open 10:00–12:30 and 15:00–18:30 mid-March to late September) was also built, with a number of impressive rooms. You can see, for instance, the bedroom where Napoleon and Josephine slept in 1797, rooms devoted to arms, medals and musical instruments, a library, a room full of 16th-century Flemish tapestry, and six grotto rooms decorated with shells, stones and volcanic material. Best of all is the richly decorated Great Hall. Many of the rooms have valuable paintings and frescoes, while nearly all have the most dazzling Murano glass chandeliers. Try to join a tour, as the guides are famously witty.

SOUTH OF STRESA

There is ribbon development along the lake shore south of Stresa, with the settlements of **Belgirate**, **Lesa**, which

Left: *Part of the historic town of Arona, protected by a Borromeo fortress.* **Opposite:** *The massive statue of San Carlo Borromeo towers over the southern end of Lake Maggiore.*

has a ruined medieval castle, and **Meina**. The first town of any size, however, is **Arona**. A strategic route centre and market town, it was protected by a Borromeo fortress, or *rocca*, but it is now in ruins as it was dismantled by Napoleon. Head for the attractive little Piazza del Populo, where the 15th-century Casa del Podestà has an arched portico. Also in the square is the 16th-century church of Madonna di Piazza. Two other churches that are worth a look are Santa Maria, which has a Borromeo family chapel, and Santi Martiri, with delightful 16th-century stained-glass windows. Most people come to Arona, however, to see the enormous **Statue of San Carlo Borromeo**, the famous 16th-century Archbishop of Milan.

THE LOMBARDY SHORE OF LAKE MAGGIORE

Although far quieter than the Piedmont side of the lake, the eastern shore does, however, have plenty to see.

Angera

Opposite Arona is the small town of Angera, dominated by the **Rocca di Angera**, a castle built initially by the Lombards on Roman foundations. Considering that it was fought over by the Franks, the Torrianis and the Viscontis before finally being taken by the Borromeos, it is in remarkably good condition. There are a number of frescoes inside, mainly glorifying the victories of the Viscontis, plus

ANGERA'S DOLL MUSEUM

The castle at Angera near the southern point of Lake Maggiore has seen much fierce fighting. It was successively a stronghold of the Lombards, the Viscontis and the Borromeos. It comes as a surprise, therefore, to see that this now houses, of all things, a **doll museum**, with a comprehensive collection of Italian dolls ranging from the late 18th century through to the modern dolls of today. As well as viewing the immaculately preserved items, it is also possible to buy dolls from one of Italy's finest doll-makers.

an unusual doll museum (*see* panel, page 77). The castle and museum are open 09:30–12:30 and 14:00–18:00 daily Easter–October (15:00–19:00 during July and August).

THE ORIGINS OF SANTA CATERINA DEL SASSO

There is an interesting story about the founding of the Monastery of Santa Caterina. It is said that in the 12th century a man of somewhat dubious character called Alberto Bessozi was sailing on the lake when a sudden storm capsized his boat. He prayed to Santa Caterina that if he could be saved he would dedicate the rest of his life to the worship of God. He was indeed saved when a wave then washed him up onto a rock ledge and, as he promised, he spent the rest of his life on this rock in prayer. Here he was kept alive by being fed by local people, whom he repaid by praying successfully for their deliverance from the plague. After he died, 39 years later, the community built a chapel on the spot and in the 14th century the Dominican monastery that we see today was built there.

Santa Caterina del Sasso

A few kilometres north of Angera is the former Dominican monastery of **Santa Caterina del Sasso**. Perched on a cliff face 18m (59ft) above the water, it can only be seen from the lake and is a regular stop for boats. If arriving by car, be prepared for a series of steep steps from the car park to the monastery. The original chapel to Santa Caterina had a monastery added in the 13th century. The monastery was suppressed by Joseph II of Austria in 1770 and was deserted for two centuries, but after a 15-year period of restoration it was reopened in 1987. There are numerous frescoes to see, varying in age from the 14th to the 17th centuries, but it is the setting that will appeal most to visitors.

Laveno

Around the headland from the monastery is the port of **Laveno**. The only natural harbour on the lake, it was an important Roman settlement and later an Austrian naval base. Today, its car ferry runs across to Intra on the Piedmont side of the lake. Laveno was well known for its ceramics industry, but this finally closed down in 1980.

You can, however, visit the **Ceramics Museum** (open 10:00–12:00 and 14:30–18:00 Friday, Saturday and Sunday, all year) which is full of items such as bizarrely decorated toilet seats and bidets. If you are in Laveno at Christmas time, don't miss the floodlit underwater nativity scene set up by local divers. The more adventurous could take the chair lift up to **Sasso del Ferro**. At 1062m (3483ft), it provides fine views of the lake and the Alps.

Luino

The next place of any size is **Luino**. It has a long history going back to Roman days but in more recent times it was famous as the place where, in 1848, Garibaldi's small band of men defeated an entire Austrian detachment, thereby speeding up the unification of the country. Luino is believed to have been the birthplace of Bernardino Luini, the most important of Leonardo's followers. One of his frescoes can be seen in the **Oratorio di Santi Pietro e Paolo**. The sleepy town really comes to life on Wednesdays when the weekly market is held in Piazza Garibaldi.

Maccagno

The only other settlement of any size before you reach the Swiss border is **Maccagno**. It is actually one of the oldest settlements on the lake, but very quiet today. It makes a good base for walks in the nearby Val Veddasca, which can be followed all the way into Switzerland.

LAKE ORTA

The most westerly of the Italian lakes, Lake Orta is also one of the smallest, measuring just 13.5km (8.5 miles) in length. It is the only lake that is wholly in Piedmont, and its outlet river, the Nigoglia, is the only one that

NOT FOR THE NERVY

There are a number of chair lifts and cable cars around Lake Maggiore, taking visitors effortlessly up to higher altitudes to appreciate the wonderful scenery. The most exciting, without doubt, is the lift from Laveno to the peak of Sasso del Ferro. The visitor does not travel in a chair, but in a two-person yellow bucket, which rises over the woods, meadows and rocks to the 1062m (3485ft) peak. If this is not enough for the more adventurous traveller, parascending and paragliding are on offer at the top of the bucket lift.

Opposite: *The Rocco di Angera, built by the Lombards, today houses a doll museum.*

Below: *Regular passenger boats run from Omegna to link all the settlements along the shores of Lake Orta.*

FACTS ABOUT LAKE ORTA

Length: 13.5km (8.38 miles).
Maximum width: 2.5km
(1.5 miles).
Maximum depth: 143m
(469ft).
Height above sea level:
290m (951ft).

runs northwards towards the Alps rather than south-wards to join the Po. The package tour industry has not homed in on Lake Orta to any great extent, although it is a popular day-trip destination. The main attraction on the lake is the small town of Orta San Giulio and the Island of San Giulio just offshore.

There are a number of attractive villages around Lake Orta, including **Pettenasco**, with a pretty lakeside front-age, **Armeno**, famous for producing an extraordinary number of chefs, and **Gozzano**, with its 4th-century bell tower. At **Vacciago** there is a 17th-century villa that was the home of the artist Antonio Calderara (1903–78). His house now contains the **Collezione Calderara** (open 10:00–12:00 and 15:00–18:00 Tuesday–Sunday May–October), which includes not only Calderara's work but also paintings by a host of other artists. Nearby is **San Maurizio d'Opaglio**, once the household tap-making capital of Italy (*see* panel on page 83).

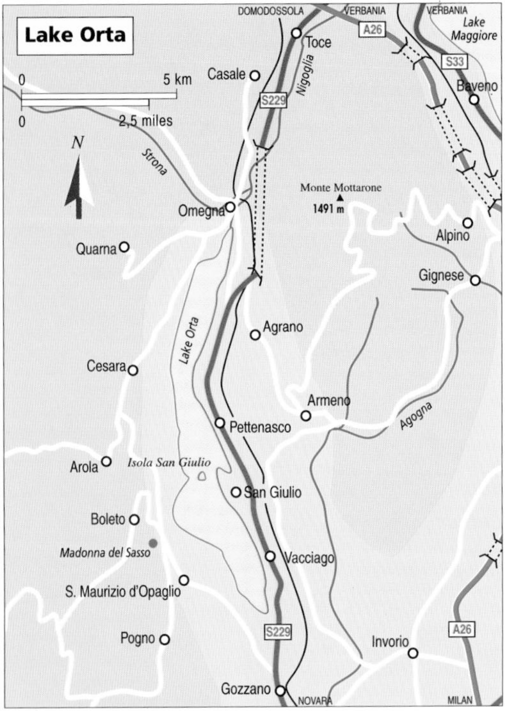

Lake Orta

Omegna

The only town of any size on Lake Orta is **Omegna**, located on the Nigoglia River at the northern end of the lake. An industrial town, it sees few tourists despite having an attract-ive tree-lined waterfront backed by graceful houses with pretty wrought-iron balconies. There is also an attractive square looking over the river and the re-mains of a bridge that is possibly Roman. There is a lively lakeside market here on Thursdays.

Although it is perfectly possible to drive around the lake to visit Orta San Giulio, it is far more enjoyable to take the lake steamer from Omegna, stopping at several lakeside villages en route.

Above: *The town hall (Palazzo della Communità) on the Piazza Morta in Orta San Giulio.*

Orta San Giulio **

This small lakeside town is a gem of a place. A diminutive square, **Piazza Morta**, is right next to the main landing stage and surrounded by bars and *gelaterie*. In among these pavement cafés is the little town hall, the **Palazzo della Communità**. It is decorated with frescoes dating back to 1582 and has an arcaded loggia. An outside staircase leads to the upper floors and a tiny campanile. Leading back from the square are narrow alleyways full of restaurants, craft shops and boutiques. Look, too, for the tower of **Villa Crespi**, the house of a newspaper owner who employed Turkish stonemasons. Prayers from the Koran can be seen on the tower of the villa, which is now a hotel. A steep cobbled road leads up to the yellow frontage of the **Church of Madonna del Sasso**, which dates from the 15th century, although it had a major restoration 300 years later. The interior is noteworthy for its strangely sloping nave floor and its impressive frescoes. On the right-hand side of the church, a steep lane leads up to **Sacro Monte**, the sacred hill with a collection of 21 chapels dedicated to St Francis of Assisi. Even if the chapels are of little interest, it is worth the walk for the stupendous views over the lake and island of San Giulio.

Isola San Giulio ***

Every 15 minutes or so, boats leave from the landing stage at Piazza Morta for Isola San Giulio. Dominating the island is the **basilica** (open 09:30–12:15 and 14:00–

THE STORY OF SAN GIULIO

In the 4th century, Giulio, a Roman missionary, decided that the island on Lake Orta would be an ideal base for his work. The local inhabitants, however, refused to row him to the island as they believed it to be the haunt of dragons and other nasty beasts. Undeterred, Giulio went across the water in the wind, standing on his cloak and using his staff as a rudder – surely the world's first windsurfer! Not surprisingly, the dragons fled on seeing such extraordinary behaviour and Giulio was able to settle on the island and devote himself to converting the Orta natives to Christianity.

**FACTS ABOUT THE
VARESE LAKES**

Lake Varese
Length: 8.5km (5.3 miles).
Width: 3.5km (2.2 miles).

Lake Comabbio
Length: 3km (2 miles).
Width: 1km (0.6 miles).

Lake Monate
Length: 2.75km (1.7 miles).
Width: 1km (0.6 miles).

Right: *A steep, cobbled
road leads to the Church
of Madonna del Sasso,
from where there are fine
views of Lake Orta and
Isola San Giulio.*

ORTA'S SACRED MOUNTAIN

The idea of **sacri monti** –
sacred hills – was brought
to Italy by a Franciscan friar,
Bernardino Caimi, after his
pilgrimage to Jerusalem.
Orta's **Sacro Monte** was
begun in 1591 and dedicated
to St Francis. It took over 200
years to build the 21 chapels
with their 376 statues and
over 900 frescoes. The route
passes through shady woods
and provides superb views
over the lake and Isola San
Giulio. People found that
this was an excellent picnic
spot and this eventually
encouraged a small bar and
restaurant to open, so that
the Sacro Monte is now a
very popular weekend venue.

18:45 daily) which was originally built around the 9th
century on the site of the hermit San Giulio's cell. Much
of the present church dates from a major rebuilding in
the 11th century. Of great interest is the large black
pulpit decorated with mythical beasts. There are also
some 15th-century frescoes (they were evacuated to the
Vatican during World War II) and a large vertebra in the
sacristy, said to come from one of the dragons that San
Giulio chased off the island, but in all probability it is a
whale bone. A cobbled alleyway runs around the island,
much of which is taken up with the monastery, but there
are a few private houses, a restaurant and a shop.

LAKE VARESE AND AROUND

West of the city of Varese and southeast of Lake
Maggiore are a trio of small lakes. The largest is **Lake
Varese**, some 9km (5.5 miles) long and surrounded by
low rolling hills and forests. Sadly, the lake is badly
polluted, so that swimming and some water sports
have been banned, while the fishing industry has all
but disappeared. In the south of the lake is the tiny
Isolino Virginia, which is largely made up of the
remains of pile-built lake dwellings going back to
Neolithic times. Artefacts collected from the site can be
seen in the museum in Varese. The two smaller lakes,
Lake Comabbio and **Lake Monate**, also have examples
of Bronze-Age pile dwellings.

The city of **Varese** has ancient origins, but today its
parks and gardens give it a 'garden city' atmosphere. It
is increasingly becoming a dormitory suburb of Milan
and its hotels take the overflow of visitors when Milan
holds its trade fairs. It has a small amount of light
industry, particularly shoe-making. There is much to
see in Varese. Pride of place goes to the **Palazzo
Estense**, a mid-18th-century Baroque palace, surrounded by extensive gardens. Once the home of the
Duke of Modena, it is now the city's town hall. Nearby
is the **Villa Mirabello**, which houses the **Musei Civici**,
with a jumbled collec-
tion of local archae-
ology, paintings and
natural history. Also
of interest here is the
Basilica of San Vittore
with its neoclassical
façade and some mildly
interesting artwork.
Next to the basilica is
Varese's landmark, the
72m (236ft) **Campanile
del Bernascone**, which is
capped with an onion-
shaped dome.

> ### MUSEUM OF TAPS
>
> There are some strange
> subjects for museums in
> the Lake Maggiore region.
> The Umbrella Museum at
> Gignese, the Chimney
> Sweep Museum at Santa
> Maria Maggiore and the Hat
> Museum at Ghiffa readily
> spring to mind. Probably
> the most bizarre is the Tap
> Museum – Museo de la
> Rubinetta – at San Maurizio
> d'Opaglio. The area was once
> famous for the manufacture
> of bathroom fittings, particu-
> larly luxury items such as the
> gold taps much favoured by
> wealthy Arabs. Today, the
> industry has largely moved to
> Brescia, but the memorabilia
> can still be seen in the
> Museum of Taps.

Below: *An attractive
flower-bedecked corner of
the pretty town of Orta
San Giulio.*

Lakes Maggiore, Orta and Varese at a Glance

In **winter** many of the attractions and monuments close from October–March. In **summer** the popular resorts can get overcrowded and the roads jammed with cars. The best time to visit is in late **spring**, when the azaleas and rhododendrons are in bloom and the botanical gardens are looking their best. **September** is also a good time as the high summer temperatures have dropped and the crowds have gone.

Trains from Milan's Stazione Centrale stop at Arona and Stresa, while the service from Milan's Porta Garibaldi serves the eastern side of Lake Maggiore. Trains from Switzerland arrive via the Simplon Tunnel to Domodossala or via the Swiss town of Bellinzona. The **road** route from Milan is simple, using the A8 and the A26 *autostradas*.

Roads follow the shores of both Lake Maggiore and Lake Orta and a car is convenient for getting to many of the attractions. **Railways** run along the eastern and western sides of Lake Maggiore, but not the northern shore. **Lake steamers**, mostly run by *Navagazione Lago Maggiore*, link all major resorts, although services are cut considerably

in winter. Hydrofoils provide an especially quick link. The only car ferry across the lake runs from Intra to Laveno.

There is a wide range of accommodation – from some of the most luxurious hotels around, down to humble *pensiones* and camp sites. All are likely to be fully booked during peak season, particularly those hotels that are popular with tour groups. Pre-booking at this time of the year is strongly recommended.

LUXURY

Grand Hotel des Iles Borromées, corso Umberto I 31, Stresa, tel: 0323 30431, fax: 0323 32405. It would be hard to better this lakeside edifice in terms of service, facilities and ambience.
Bristol, corso Umberto I 75, Stresa, tel: 0323 32601, fax: 0323 33622. Another of Stresa's luxurious lakeside hotels, with indoor and outdoor pools and gym.
La Palma, corso Umberto I 1, Stresa, tel: 0323 32401, fax: 0323 933 930. Modern hotel with pool across the road by the lake. Good restaurant.
Dino, via Garibaldi 20, Baveno, tel: 0323 922 201, fax: 0323 924 515. Luxury hotel with private lakeside beach.
Majestic, via Vittorio Veneto 32, Pallanza, tel: 0323 504 305, fax: 0323 556 379. Comfortable older-style hotel

with excellent facilities and private beach.

MID-RANGE

Sasso Moro, in hamlet of Arolo di Leggiuno, 7km (4.3 miles) south of Laveno, tel: 0332 64730. Quiet hotel with a fine waterside location.
Park Hotel Paradiso, via Guglielmo Marconi 20, Ghiffa, tel: 0323 59548, fax: 0323 59878. Small hotel in Art Nouveau villa with pool and good views.
Rigoli, via Piave 48, Baveno, tel: 0323 924 756, fax: 0323 925 156. Lakeside; stunning views in all directions.
Cannero, 28821 Cannero Riviera, tel: 0323 788 046, fax: 0323 788 048. Rooms with balconies overlooking the lake. Swimming pool. Good restaurant.
Pironi, via Marconi 35, Cannobio, tel: 0323 70624, fax: 0323 72184. Comfortable hotel in 15th-century palace.
Dell'Angelo, Piazza Grande, Locarno, Switzerland, tel: (41) 91 751 8175, fax: 751 8256. Large rooms, roof terrace and cheap pizzeria.

BUDGET

Pensione l'Isola, via Rebolgiane 68, Laveno, tel: 0332 666 031. Reasonably priced, in the centre of town.
Elena, piazza Cadorna 15, Stresa, tel: 0323 31043, fax: 0323 33339. Excellent budget choice in the main square. Large rooms with balconies.

Lakes Maggiore, Orta and Varese at a Glance

Orsola, via Duchessa di Genova 45, Stresa, tel: 0323 31087. Comfortable, good value, close to train station.
Olina, via Olina 40, Orta San Giulio, tel: 0322 905 656, fax: 0322 905 645. A rare cheap option in this popular town. Good reasonable restaurant.

There are plenty of **camp sites** around and they include:
Lido, on the lakeside at Arona, tel: 0322 243 383.
Parisi, via Piave 50, Baveno, tel: 0323 923 156. Open Apr–Sep.
La Residence, Cannobio, close to the river. Open Mar–Oct. Also has some rooms in a nearby villa.
Lido, waterfront at Maccagno, tel: 0332 560 250.

WHERE TO EAT

Some of the most stylish restaurants are to be found in the main hotels, but often the food is bland and inter-national. The towns around the lakes have few 'foreign' restaurants, such as Chinese or Mexican. Most serve Italian regional food, with an emphasis on traditional local fish dishes.

LUXURY
Taverna del Pittore, piazza del Popolo 39, Arona, tel: 0322 243 366. One of the top restaurants on Lake Maggiore, with fine views from its terrace over the lake and the Rocca. Bring a bulging wallet.

Centenario, lungolago Motta 17, Locarno, Switzerland, tel: (41) 91 743 8222. Top restaurant noted for its gourmet food.
L'Emiliano, corso Italia 52, Stresa, tel: 0323 31396. Nouvelle cuisine, imaginative dishes and very expensive.

MID-RANGE
Campanile, via Montegrappa 16, Baveno, tel: 0323 922 377. Classic pasta dishes.
Torchio, via Manzoni 25, Stresa, tel: 0323 503 352. Good value game dishes.
Verbano, Isola dei Pescatori, tel: 0323 30408. Good fish restaurant on the east of the island overlooking Isola Bella.
Osteria dell'Angelo, piazza Garibaldi 35, Pallanza, tel: 0323 556 362. Well known for its imaginative risottos.
Lo Scalo, piazza Lago 32, Cannobio, tel: 0323 71480. Traditional Piedmontese recipes enjoyed from a terrace overlooking the lake.

BUDGET
For the standard cheap meal go to **Panini** bars, which offer a variety of sandwiches in different types of bread.
Pizzerias are another possi-bility. Many bars in the main resorts offer cheap snack food.

SHOPPING

Most resorts have a street market on one day of the week. Bargains can be found in leather goods and shoes.

TOURS AND EXCURSIONS

The numerous **cable cars** and **chair lifts** are popular with tourists. Nobody should leave Lake Maggiore without visiting the **Borromean Islands**, which are easy to reach on the local ferries. Favourite excursions with the tour operators are to the Alpine village of **Macugnaga** and the **Hundred Valleys** rail trip.

USEFUL CONTACTS

A list of **Tourist Information Offices** is shown below. Most are run by APT, others by local municipalities. For more information visit the website: www.lagomaggiore.it
Stresa, via Canonica 8, tel: 0323 31308. They will give details of the Stresa International Festival of Classical Music.
Baveno, pizziale Dante Alighieri 14, tel: 0323 924 632.
Cannobio, via Marconi 4, tel: 0323 71212.
Luino, viale Dante 6, tel: 0332 530 019.
Orta San Giulio, Via Panoramica, tel: 0322 905 614.
Varese, viale Ippodromo 9, tel: 0332 284 624.
Locarno, Lago Zorzi 1, tel: (41) 91 751 0333.
Ascona, Casa Seradine, tel: (41) 91 791 0090.

For details of ferry times tel: 0322 46651.

5
Lakes Como and Lugano

Lake Como, which is also known by the Roman name of Lario, is the third largest lake in Italy, stretching for around 50km (32 miles) from north to south. It is also believed to be the deepest lake in Europe, glaciers having scoured it out to a depth of 410m (1345ft). The lake takes the form of an inverted Y, its three arms known as Como, Lecco and Cólico. Lake Como is the only northern Italian lake to have a major city on its shore, the ancient town of Como, with its defensive walls largely intact, historically guarding the north–south and east–west routes.

Como is generally considered to be the most attractive and romantic of the northern lakes. Picture-perfect lakeside villages, sumptuous villas such as **Villa Carlotta** and **Villa d'Este**, and exotic gardens prolific with blooms attracted English poets including Wordsworth, Shelley and Byron. Royalty followed and Lake Como soon began to be an important part of the 19th-century Grand Tour.

Today, unfortunately, Como is also the most crowded of the lakes. In the summer its waters are dotted with a wide variety of crafts from sailboards to hydrofoils, while the perimeter roads can be clogged with traffic. Como is the nearest of the northern lakes to Milan, and the Milanese arrive in hordes at the weekends and during the holiday month of August. Yet somehow the essential attractiveness of Lake Como is never quite ruined by the crowds, and it remains a fabulous holiday destination.

DON'T MISS

*** Villa Carlotta: 18th-century neoclassical lakeside villa at Tremezzo.
*** Como's Duomo: the magnificent cathedral shows transitional architecture from Gothic to Renaissance.
** Villa d'Este: 16th-century villa at Cernobbio, now a luxury hotel.
** Bellagio: often described as the prettiest village on the Italian lakes.
* Funicular to Brunate:. superb views over Como and the lake from the top of the funicular railway at Brunate.

Opposite: *The Villa d'Este has a long history and is now a luxury hotel.*

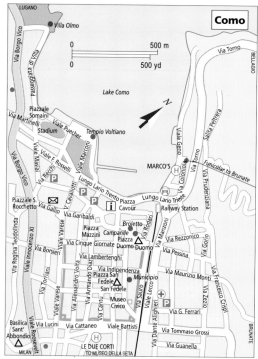

COMO

The city of Como, at the tip of the southwest arm of the lake, has had a long and eventful history. The first settlement was probably in the Bronze Age, but it became important during Roman times, when Julius Caesar brought settlers to the site. The Romans recognized the strategic importance of Como and linked it by road to Milan. It later came under the rule of the Viscontis and then the Sforzas, when it became very prosperous, its wealth based on silk and other textiles. The Spanish rule marked a period of decline, but it picked up later during the Habsburg and Napoleonic occupations. Como was prominent during the *Risorgimento*, and after Garibaldi defeated the Austrians at the Battle of San Fermo, his troops were received enthusiastically in the city.

Today Como has a population of 100,000 and its prosperity is based on textiles, engineering and tourism. Despite some industrial suburbs, its historical core is attractive, with a street plan intact from the days of the Roman *castrum* and its medieval walls in good condition.

Life in the city today centres on the **Piazza Cavour**, which opens out onto the lakeside promenade with its gardens and landing stages, enabling boat passengers to disembark in the heart of the city. It is a lively square, backed by hotels and cafés. From Piazza Cavour, Via Plinio leads inland to **Piazza Duomo**, with the cathedral, Broletto (the striped marble town hall) and a Campanile.

LAKE COMO'S CLIMATE

Lake Como has a mild, almost frost-free climate that enables a variety of exotic plants to grow and thrive. The **summer** can be hot, particularly in August, when thunderstorms are not uncommon. **Spring** is the best time of the year for sightseeing, with many plants and shrubs in full flower. **Winds** can occasionally be strong, with the *breva* blowing northwards from midday to sunset, while the *tivà* blows south during the night and the early morning.

The Duomo

Como's magnificent cathedral was begun in 1396 and eventually completed in 1744. It is regarded as a superb example of the transition from Gothic to Renaissance. The two ends of the cathedral present contrasts in the two styles of architecture. The east end is pure Renaissance, with green-roofed apses, matching the Baroque dome that was added by Filipo Juvarra in 1744. The flat western façade is largely Gothic, its polished marble setting off the long narrow windows and numerous statues. On either side of the main west door are statues of the Elder and Younger Plinys who were both born in Como (but in the days when the Roman Empire was pagan). The statues were the work of the Rodari brothers, who were also responsible for the ornate north door (facing the Broletto) known as the Porta della Rana or Frog Door.

The interior is equally interesting, with three Gothic aisles sitting happily with the Renaissance transepts and choir. Don't miss the hanging tapestries between four columns of the nave. They date from the 16th and 17th centuries and originated in Tuscany and Flanders. Note also the rose window with fine stained glass, the paintings by Gaudenzio Ferrari and Bernardino Luini, and the Romanesque lions near the main entrance, which were retained from an original church on the site that was demolished to make way for the cathedral.

Attached to the north side of the Duomo is the **Broletto** which dates from 1215. Two of its arches were removed when the cathedral was built. Alongside the Broletto is the **Campanile**, made contrastingly of rough-hewn stone.

PLINY AND PLINY

The famous Romans, Pliny the Elder and Pliny the Younger, were both natives of Como. Pliny the Elder was a notable Latin prose writer who became a government servant. His most famous work was his *Natural History*, a comprehensive book dealing with the world's geography, biology, geology and medicine. He died inhaling the fumes from the eruption of Vesuvius at Pompeii. Pliny the Younger was the nephew and adopted son of Pliny the Elder. He was also a prose writer and became a Roman senator. Although both were pagan, their statues can be found on either side of the west door of Como's cathedral.

Piazza San Fedele ★

Head deeper into the old town of Como to the cobbled **Piazza San Fedele**, the site of the old corn market. Dominating the square is the 10th-century **Basilica of San Fedele**, built on the site of a pagan temple to Jupiter. Much of the work on the basilica was carried

Below: *The cafés in Como's Piazza Duomo are convenient for viewing the cathedral.*

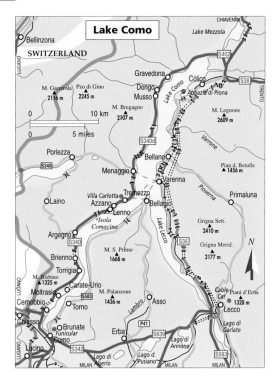

Lake Como

CHIAVENNA
Lake Mezzola
Bellinzona
SWITZERLAND
LUGANO
Gravedona
Colico
M. Garzirola   Pzo di Gino   Dongo
2116 m   2245 m   Musso   Abbazia di Piona
M. Bregagno
M. Legnone
2107 m   2609 m
0   10 km
0   5 miles
Varrone
Porlezza   S340d
Bellano
Menaggio   Pian d. Betulle
1456 m
Varenna
Villa Carlotta Tremezzo
Azzano   Proverna
Laino   Lenno   Bellagio   Primaluna
Isola
Comacina   Grigna Sett.
2410 m
Argegno   S340
Lago Lecco   Grigna Merid.
M. S. Primo   2177 m
Brienno   1668 m
Torriggia
M. Bisbino   Carate-Urio   Cable
1325 m   M. Palanzone   Car   Piani d'Erna
Moltrasio   S583   1436 m   Asso   1328 m
Cernobbio   Torno   Lecco
Chiasso   Lambro   Lago di
Brunate   Erba   Garlate
Lucino   Funicular   P41   Lago di
Como   Annone
S342   Lago di   Lago d.   S583
MILAN   Alserio   Pusiano   MILAN   MILAN

N

FACTS ABOUT LAKE COMO

Como is the third largest of
the Italian lakes. It has the
longest shoreline of all the
lakes and is one of the
deepest lakes in Europe,
having been scoured out by
glacial action.
Length: 50km (32 miles).
Maximum width: 4.4km
(2.7 miles).
Area: 148km² (55 sq miles).
Perimeter: 170km (106
miles).
Maximum depth: 410m
(1345ft) near Argegno.

out by the *Maestri Como-cini*, the area's famous master builders and stone-masons. One of the best features of San Fedele is the exterior of the apse, with its upper arcade and round windows decorated with Romanesque bas-reliefs. Como's other fine church is the Romanesque **Sant'Abbondio**, built in the 11th century and boasting some colourful 14th-century frescoes.

Museums

Como has three museums worth a visit. A short walk from San Fedele is the **Museo Civico**, housed in two palaces. The **Palazzo Olginati** has the *Risorgimento* museum, with plenty of Garibaldi memorabilia, while the **Palazzo Giovio** keeps the local collection of archaeology and art. Open 09:30–12:30 and 14:00–17:00 Tuesday–Saturday; 10:00–13:00 Sunday.

A rather special museum is the **Tempio Voltiano** in the lakeside park. The circular building was erected in 1927 to house the instruments and papers of Como's famous self-taught scientist, Alessandro Volta, who gave his name to the electrical measurement (*see* panel, page 93). The museum is open 10:00–12:00 and 15:00–18:00 Tuesday–Sunday, April–September; 10:00–12:00 and 14:00–16:00 Tuesday–Sunday, October–March.

The **Museo della Seta**, located in Via Vallegio to the south of the historic centre of Como, charts the history of the city's silk industry. Open 09:00–12:00 and 15:00–18:00 Tuesday–Friday.

Villa Olmo *

At night, you can't miss the floodlit **Villa Olmo**. In formal neoclassical style, it was built on the site of a monastery in the late 18th century. Its manicured formal gardens are open to the public (09:00–19:00 in winter, 08:00–23:00 in summer). A couple of the rooms in the villa can be visited (09:30–12:00 and 15:00–18:00 Monday–Saturday) if they are not being used for conferences.

The Funicular to Brunate **

Do not leave Como without taking the funicular to Brunate. The service runs every 30 minutes from the lakeside station to the hill village. For superb views over Como and the lake, walk down the road from the upper station for 100m (110yd), or take the panoramic footpath in the opposite direction for 500m (666yd). Brunate is also a good starting point for hikes in the surrounding hills. A clutch of cheap restaurants and pizzerias alongside the upper station make this a good lunchtime stop.

Above: *The Villa d'Este is a luxury hotel with magnificent landscaped gardens.*

THE WESTERN SHORE OF LAKE COMO

The suburbs of Como extend along the western shore to **Cernobbio**, the third largest town on the lake. Although there is light industry on the outskirts, Cernobbio has a pleasant waterfront leading back to a small square, the site of a popular market on Wednesdays and Saturdays. There is also a lakeside lido nearby. Cernobbio is the start of a 130km (80-mile) trek through the mountains along the western shore of Como known as the **Via dei Monte Lariani**. The town is best known, however, for its sumptuous villas, which include **Villa Erba**, now an exhibition and conference centre, **Villa Il Pizzo** with its beautiful gardens, and the world-famous late 16th-century **Villa d'Este**, now a luxury hotel.

FROM VILLA TO LAVISH HOTEL

The **Villa d'Este** at Cernobbio was built in 1568 as the summer residence of Cardinal Tolomeo Gallio, who was Pope Gregory XIII's Secretary of State. It remained in the family's hands until the 19th century when it became the home of Caroline of Brunswick, exiled wife of the Prince of Wales, (who was later George IV). In 1873 Villa d'Este became a luxury hotel, and over the years it has accommodated a long list of royalty and celebrities, from the Duke of Windsor and Mrs Simpson to Greta Garbo and Madonna.

The road north passes along one of the most attractive stretches of Lake Como, with a series of tunnels and glimpses of the blue waters of the lake and the far shore. There is a string of villages including **Moltrasio**, where the Villa Passalacqua was a favourite stop for the composer Bellini; **Carate-Urio**, above which is the 10th-century **Santuario de Santa Maria**, giving fine views across the lake; **Torrigia,** and **Brienno**.

Eventually you will reach **Argegno**. It is a pleasant village, with lakeside cafés and wooden-beamed houses almost covering the stepped alleyways running between them. The Val d'Intelvi, inland from Argegno, is drained by the River Telo, which rushes under an old bridge believed to be of Roman origin. A winding narrow road follows the valley inland and over the hills to Lake Lugano. Try the *funvia* that runs up to the hamlet of Pigra at a height of 881m (2890ft), giving stunning views over the lake.

THE TREMEZZINA

The next stretch of the lake is known as the Tremezzina, a sheltered area with lush vegetation and a gentle climate. Offshore is Como's only island, **Isola Comacina**. Full of ruined churches, its only inhabitants are a small colony of artists. It can be reached by ferry, but its only restaurant is one of the priciest around the lake. The first village of the Tremezzina is **Lenno**, where Pliny the Younger had a villa. He wrote that he could fish from his bedroom window. The next village, **Azzano**, has more recent historical fame, for it was here that Mussolini and his mistress were executed by partisans in 1945.

The main resort of this stretch of the lake shore is the romantic **Tremezzo**, which looks across towards Bellagio at the junction of the three arms of Lake Como. A string

---

CENTRE OF SILK PRODUCTION

In the 17th century, the production of silk moved from Milan to Como and within a short time the area was providing fine silk to the royal courts in many parts of Europe. The mulberry bushes, on which silkworms were raised, were a common sight along the lake. In the 19th century disaster struck when an epidemic wiped out all the Como silkworms. The industry survived by importing raw silk from China. Today, the industry flourishes, producing 80 per cent of Europe's silk, and is the major source of the fine silk fabrics that the Milan fashion industry demands. The development of the industry can be seen in the **Museo della Seta** (Silk Museum) in Como.

of opulent palaces and villas, many of which have been converted into hotels, line the shore. One of these, the **Villa Carlotta**, is one of the main tourist attractions of the Italian lakes. It was built in the 18th century in neo-classical style by Marchese Giorgio Clerici and in the following century came into the hands of Princess Carlotta of the Netherlands. The interior of the villa is full of fascinating works of art, but it is the gardens, with their azaleas, rhododendrons and camellias, that will probably leave a more lasting impression. Villa Carlotta is open 09:00–11:30 and 14:00–16:30 daily from 15 March to 31 October; 09:00–18:00 daily from April to September.

Menaggio, the next resort, is the busiest of the towns on the western shore. A car ferry connects it to the eastern shore at Varenna, while a road leads westward to Lugano and Switzerland just 12km (7.5 miles) away. Menaggio is a lively resort with a good beachside lido, golf course, stylish shops, attractive harbour and a number of good hotels.

After a string of small hamlets, the town of **Musso** is reached. It is defended by a castle built on the Sasso di Musso, which was once the home of Il Medighino, a member of the Medici who terrorized the lake for many years during the 16th century. The quarries in the hills behind Musso provided the marble for Como's Duomo and also the Arch of Peace in Milan. Just north of Musso is **Dongo**, the place where Mussolini was captured by partisans in 1945 while attempting to flee to Switzerland in a German lorry.

The last town of any size on the western shore is **Gravedona**. The oldest town on the lake after Como, it has two main monuments. The **Palazzo Gallio** was built in 1586 for Cardinal Tolemeo Gallio and today it operates as the offices of the local council. The **Church**

ALESSANDRO VOLTA (1745–1827)

Volta was born in Como, where he became a school-teacher. He published several papers on electricity and magnetism, and as a result of his skill he was made Professor of Physics at Padua University. He is best known for inventing the voltaic pile, which was the first example of an electric battery of primary cells, and also for his development of the theory of current electricity. When he retired, he returned to Como, where there are a street and a square (with his statue) named after him. The pupose-built **Tempio Voltiano** (see page 90) on the lake shore contains an exhibition of his manuscripts and apparatus.

Opposite: *The Villa Carlotta was named after a Dutch princess. Don't miss its fine gardens.*
Below: *The waterfront at Menaggio, the tourist resort on the western shore.*

COMO'S ONLY ISLAND

Just off the Tremezzo coast is Lake Como's only island, **Isola Comacina**. This tiny island, measuring just 800m x 400m (875yd x 437yd), has, nevertheless, a fascinating history. It was first inhabited by the Romans, but achieved its pinnacle of power in the 12th century, when it supported Milan in its fight against Como. Later it was sacked by Como, with hardly a building left intact. It was then abandoned for centuries until, after World War II, it was bought by the king of the Belgians. The king eventually returned the island to the Italian state, which built three houses there for the use of Milanese artists. Apart from these houses, a church and a very expensive restaurant, there are only ruins left on Isola Comacina.

of **Santa Maria del Tiglio** dates from the 12th century and is believed to have been built over the remains of an earlier Roman church. It has an attractive aisled nave where you will find a 6th-century mosaic floor and some frescoes dating from the 12th–14th centuries. There is also an ancient wooden crucifix.

At the extreme northern end of Lake Como is the tiny **Lake Mezzola**, measuring just 3km by 2km (2 miles by 1.25 miles). Once part of the main lake, it became detached by the build-up of silt and boulders deposited by the rivers Mera and Adda. The surrounding reed beds and marsh land provide a haven for wildfowl.

THE EASTERN SHORE OF LAKE COMO

The first village of any size and the last northerly stop of the lake steamers is **Cólico**, but this has little to detain visitors. Just to the south, however, is a small lagoon known as the **Lago di Piona**, and on the finger of land that encloses the lagoon is a restored 11th-century abbey, the **Abbazia di Piona**. The abbey was taken over by the Cistercians in the early years of the 20th century and today it is open daily to visitors from 08:00–19:00. The abbey has some particularly attractive mid-13th-century cloisters and an imposing campanile.

Further south is **Bellano**, the home of the Boldini family who were credited with introducing the silk industry to the Como region. Bellano seems to successfully combine a little light industry with a tourist trade. Its most impressive monument is the **Church of San Nazzaro and San Celso**. Dating from the 14th century, it has a fine rose window and a superb marble façade. Look out too for the 16th-century *Madonna and Child*, possibly by Luini.

Behind the town is a deep gorge or *orrido*, where the River Pioverna comes crashing down the valley. It is accessible by steps and rope walkways.

Varenna **

A short distance south of Bellano is Varenna, one of the most picturesque

towns on the lake. The houses are strung out along the base of the hills and the old quarter, in particular, is an attractive maze of narrow lanes, alleyways and arches. On the hill above the town is a ruined castle, which is believed to have been the last home of the Lombard Queen Theolinda. A more recent denizen of the town was Pirelli, who founded the tyre firm.

There are two churches of interest. The **Oratorio di San Giovanni** goes back to the 10th century and is one of the oldest surviving churches on the lake. **San Giorgio** is in Romanesque style and its exterior is graced by an elegant campanile and a fresco of St Francis. Inside are some more frescoes and an altarpiece by Pietro Brentani.

There are a number of magnificent lakeside villas in Varenna, most of which have become hotels or conference centres. The most famous are **Villa Cipressi**, with terraced gardens going right down to the lakeside (open 09:00–19:00 in summer and 09:00–18:00 in autumn and spring), and **Villa Monastero**, built on the site of a Cistercian monastery and used today by the government as a scientific centre. Its gardens are well worth a visit. Open 10:00–12:00 and 14:00–18:30 from May–October. Varenna also boasts the **Museo Ornitologico**, which concentrates on the birds that have been seen around the lake. Open 15:00–18:00 Tuesday, Thursday and Saturday, June–September; 10:00–12:00 Sunday. Varenna is also an important ferry centre – a car ferry runs to Tremezzo and steamers to Bellagio, Villa Carlotta, Menaggio and most of the other lakeside resorts.

Above: *Picturesque Varenna on the eastern shore of Lake Como.*
Opposite: *Lakeside Bellano, once an important silk-producing centre.*

THE END OF MUSSOLINI

A German convoy was heading north into Switzerland on 27 April 1945. Concealed in the lorries were a number of Italian Fascist leaders, including Mussolini. Unfortunately for *Il Duce* the convoy was stopped by partisans near the lakeside resort of Dongo. While many of the Fascists were executed on the spot, Mussolini and his mistress Clara Petacci were taken south towards Milan to be tried. When they reached the hamlet of Azzano they were stopped by a local partisan leader who, for reasons best known to himself, shot Mussolini and his mistress. Their bodies continued their journey to Milan where they were strung up on a lamppost.

A SHORT-LIVED REPUBLIC

During medieval times the three towns of **Dongo**, **Sorico** and **Gravedona** formed the **Tre Pievi** (or three parishes) **Republic**, with the larger Gravedona as capital. The republic at one time ran a 'pirate ship' that terrorized the northern end of the lake. The republic itself was later terrorized by the inquisitor, Peter of Verona, as they had a stated policy which doubted that the pope was Christ's representative on earth. The feisty republic in revenge hacked Peter to death, but within a few years the three parishes had been taken over by the forces of Como.

THE LECCO ARM

The southeasterly arm of Lake Como is also known as the **Lago di Lecco**. It is the least developed part of the lake, with few settlements and fiord-like scenery. The small town of **Mandello del Lario** is backed by the **Grigna** mountain range, which rises to 2410m (7906ft). Mandello's main claim to fame these days is that it is the headquarters of the Moto Guzzi motorcycle firm, who run the **Museo del Motocicio** in Via Parodi. There are daily guided tours at 15:00. Of more ancient interest is the **Church of San Lorenzo**, which dates back to the 9th century.

Lecco

At the southern end of the lake is the industrial town of Lecco. With a population of 46,000, it is the second largest town on Lake Como. Despite the commercial activity in the town, there is much of historical interest. It is believed that there was a settlement here in prehistoric times and the remains of its fortifications go back to the 6th century. Lecco was taken over by the Viscontis, who built the **Ponte Vecchio** (or Ponte Azzone Visconti) in 1336. The bridge has recently been restored. Lecco was the birthplace of **Alessandro Manzoni**, the famous Italian novelist, and his best-known work, *I Promessi Sposi* (The Betrothed), was set in the town. His childhood home, the **Villa Manzoni** in Via Amendola, is now a museum. Open 09:30–14:00 Tuesday–Sunday. The town museum is housed in the 18th-century **Palazzo Belgioiosa** in Corso Matteotti. Open 10:00–12:30 and 14:30–17:30 Tuesday–Sunday. Just to the south of the Ponte Visconti is the old fishing quarter of **Pescarenico**, often described as the last genuine fishing village on the lake. Certainly there are plenty of the traditional boats and drying nets to see. For a good view over the town and the lake, take

Below: *Bellagio, with its many lakeside cafés, is usually considered to be the most attractive of Lake Como's resorts.*

the cable car to **Piani d'Erna** at 1328m (4360ft). This is a good start for hiking trails into the surrounding mountains.

Bellagio

A strong contender for the title of the most beautiful town in Italy, Bellagio sits prettily on the tip of the triangle of land between the two southern arms of Lake Como. Its leafy promenade is backed by attractive villas and restaurants, and leading from here is a maze of stepped and cobbled alleyways. It is worth walking up to the crest of the peninsula from where there are stunning views in all directions. There is good lake swimming to be had at the lido at the end of the promenade. **Villa Melzi** dates from 1810 and has some attractive gardens. Liszt composed some of his works here. The 16th-century **Villa Serbelloni** is perched on the hill above the town. Once popular with European monarchs, it is now owned by the Rockefeller Foundation, and JF Kennedy was once a guest here. The villa is not open to the public, but there are guided tours of the gardens, which have to be booked at the tourist office on Piazza della Chiesa. Before leaving Bellagio, take a look at the 12th-century **Church of San Giacomo**, which has a painting in the sacristy by Foppa and a pulpit with carvings of the Apostles.

LAKE LUGANO

Lake Lugano is situated largely in the Ticino canton of Switzerland, except for part of the western shore, the northeastern arm and the little enclave of Campione, which are Italian. Lake Lugano is narrower and more

---

SAILING ON LAKE COMO

The steady winds that blow on Lake Como make it a haven for sailing and windsurfing enthusiasts. From midday until sunset a keen wind known as the *breva* blows from south to north and is particularly strong in the northern arm of the lake. Windsurfing aficionados head for **Domaso**, just north of Gravedona, while the Como Sailing Club is based at **Pianello del Lario** just to the south of Dongo. It is appropriate that a **Boat Museum** is located at Pianello. Here you can see many of the traditional craft that have sailed on Lake Como over the centuries and see some of the tools that have helped to make them.

Opposite: *The charming little Church of Santa Maria degli Angioli, dating from the early 16th century.*

remote than the other lakes and has fewer developments around its shore. It does, however, have the sophisticated major city of Lugano.

The first lakeside town encountered when arriving at Lake Lugano from Lake Como, just 12km (7.5 miles) to the east, is **Porlezza**. It is a pleasant enough place, although it has little in the way of monuments, apart from a ruined church. After crossing the Swiss border, the first place of any size is **Gandria**, which has an interesting **Customs Museum**, illustrating the battle against smuggling that has gone on over the centuries. The museum is open 14:30–17:30 daily, Easter to October. From Gandria a funicular leads up to **Monte Bré** at a height of 925m (3035ft), providing superb views of the Alps and the lake.

LUGANO

Elegant Lugano has been Swiss since it was taken from Milan in 1512, but its language and flavour are still very much Italian. It has a beautiful lakeside setting, with a tree-lined promenade leading to the **Parco Ciani**. Here is **Villa Ciani**, which houses the town's art collection. Further along the lake shore at Castagnola is **Villa Favorita**, which once displayed the Thyssen-Bornemisza Old Masters art collection. These are now in Madrid and Barcelona, but it is still possible to see the family's extensive watercolour collection. Villa Favorita is open 10:00–17:00 Friday, Saturday and Sunday, April–June; 10:00–17:00 Tuesday–Sunday, July–October.

Back in Lugano, life revolves around the charming main square, **Piazza della Riforma**. On the south side of the square, flanked by fountains, is the neoclassical **town hall**. This is the location of the Tourist Information Office. Pedestrianized streets with fashionable shops lead away

---

PARADISE FOR CHOCOHOLICS

Switzerland is noted for its production of chocolate, and among the high-class shops in Lugano are a number selling mouthwatering chocolates in many shapes and forms. If your salivary glands are now working overtime, why not visit the **Chocolate Museum** at Caslano, 8km (5 miles) south-west of Lugano. The Swiss chocolate-makers, Alprose, offer a tour of their factory and museum, with, of course, an opportunity to sample the products! The museum is open 09:00–18:00 Monday–Friday, 09:00–17:00 Saturday and Sunday.

from the square. The **Duomo**, dedicated to San Lorenzo and dating from 1517, has a gracious Lombard-Venetian façade with richly carved portals. The interior has some 14th-century frescoes. More impressive than the cathedral is the **Church of Santa Maria degli Angioli**, which was built by the Franciscans in 1510. The simple interior has a large olive-wood altar and four side chapels, but it is dominated by a huge crucifixion scene with life-sized figures, painted around 1529 by Bernardo Luini, the pupil of Leonardo da Vinci. Less attractive is the lakeside model of the Chiesa San Carlo, made in wood by the unemployed. Funicular fans could take the trip from Lugano's southern suburb of Paradiso to the top of **Monte San Salvatore**, which rises to 915m (3001ft). There is a restaurant at the top and hiking trails lead off in a number of directions.

OTHER LAKESIDE PLACES

On the eastern shore is the Italian enclave of **Campione**, with a popular municipal casino. In the west, the short River Tresa drains Lake Lugano, feeding into Lake Maggiore. On either side of the river lies the town of **Ponte Tresa**, one half in Switzerland, the other half in Italy. Nearby at **Magliaso** is the popular **Zoo al Maglio**, with over a hundred species of mammals. The zoo is open 10:00–17:00 daily, with extended closing in the summer months. One of the most attractive villages on the lake is **Morcote**, located at the tip of the peninsula that leads south from Lugano. The **Church of Madonna del Sasso** has some superb 16th-century frescoes, while the lakeside **Parco Scherrer**, with its statues set among some exotic trees and shrubs, is a peaceful place to spend an hour or so. Across the lake from Morcote, set in a fairly wide bay, is the transport centre of **Porto Ceresio**.

A LITTLE BIT OF ITALY IN SWITZERLAND

The enclave of **Campione** on the eastern shore of Lake Lugano has been part of Italy since it was bequeathed to the church of Sant'Ambrogio in Milan in 777. In the Middle Ages it was famous for its master builders, the **Maestri Campionesi**, whose skills can be seen in many of the cathedrals of northern Italy. Today Campione is better known for its **casino**, which has been fleecing the Swiss of their francs since 1917.

FACTS ABOUT LAKE LUGANO

Four-fifths of Lake Lugano is situated in Switzerland, one-fifth in Italy.
Maximum length: from northeast to southwest is 36km (22 miles).
Maximum width: 2km (1.25 miles).
Largest town: Lugano.
Population: 40,000.

Lakes Como and Lugano at a Glance

BEST TIMES TO VISIT

Avoid July and August if possible, as it will be hot and crowded. Remember that in winter many monuments and attractions are closed. Late spring is probably the best time to visit, when the gardens will be at their colourful best. September is also good as the crowds have gone and the temperatures have moderated.

GETTING THERE

The nearest international **airports** are Milan Linate and Milan Malpensa. The cities of Como and Lugano can be reached by **road** using the A2/A9 *autostradas* from Milan. Lecco and the eastern side of Lake Como can be accessed using the N36. Road routes from Switzerland to the area use the St Bernard and St Gotthard tunnels and passes. Como, Lecco and Lugano are all linked to Milan by **rail**.

GETTING AROUND

The most pleasant way of getting around the lakes is by **boat**. A variety of craft are available, including car ferries, steamers, hydrofoils and hire boats. **Roads** run all the way round Lake Como and for much of the shore of Lake Lugano, so that a hire car is a useful asset. A **railway** runs the full length of the eastern shore of Lake Como, and there is also a link between Como and Lugano.

WHERE TO STAY

There are a vast number of accommodation possibilities around lakes Como and Lugano. Many of the expensive hotels can be booked up well in advance during the height of the season. Budget accommodation can be difficult to find, but the larger towns of Como and Lecco have possibilities.

LUXURY

Villa d'Este, via Regina 40, Cernobbio, tel: 031 3481, fax: 031 348 844. World-famous luxury with a long list of celebrity clients. Facilities include wonderful gardens and a swimming pool that 'floats' in the lake.

Grand Hotel Villa Sebelloni, via Roma 1, Bellagio, tel: 031 950 216, fax: 031 951 529. Luxurious villa in glorious gardens. Wide range of leisure facilities. Closed in November.

Grand Hotel Tremezzo Palace, Tremezzo, tel: 0344 42491, fax: 0344 40201. Comfortable 19th-century lakeside hotel situated next to Villa Carlotta.

Hotel Bellevue au Lac, riva Caccia 10, Lugano, Switzerland, tel: (41) 91 543 333. Comfortable large hotel with pool and sun terrace.

Le Due Corti, piazza Vittoria 12/13, Como, tel: 031 328 111, fax: 031 328 800. Hotel housed in a former monastery, with rooms around the old cloisters.

MID-RANGE

Du Lac, via del Pristino 4, Varenna, tel: 0341 830 238, fax: 0341 831 081. A 19th-century lakeside house with fabulous views from the rooms.

Florence, piazza Mazzini 46, Bellagio, tel: 031 950 342, fax: 031 951 722. Small traditional hotel on the lake shore.

Marco's, via Coloniola 43, Como, tel: 031 303 628, fax: 031 302 342. Small but comfortable hotel. Rooms with balconies.

Bella Vista, Menaggio, tel: 0344 32136, fax: 0344 31793. Lakeside hotel, comfortable rooms, good facilities.

Washington, via San Gottardo 55, Lugano, Switzerland, tel: (41) 91 966 4136, fax: 967 5067. Quiet, with attractive gardens and a recommended restaurant.

BUDGET

La Griglia, via Milano 15, Argegno, tel: 031 821 147, fax: 031 821 562. On lake front, Como's western shore.

Suisse, piazza Mazzini 8, Bellagio, tel: 031 950 335. Looks tatty on the outside, but has a good restaurant.

Villa Marie, Tremezzo, tel: 0344 40427. Clean, small hotel on the lake shore close to Villa Carlotta.

Youth Hostels

Villa Olmo, via Bellinzona 2, Como, tel: 031 573 800. Open Mar–Nov. Has laundry facilities and rents out bikes.

Lakes Como and Lugano at a Glance

Ostello La Primula, via IV Novembre 86, Menaggio, tel: 0344 32356. Open mid-Mar–mid-Nov. Good meals, rents out bikes and gives discounts on local attractions.

Camp Sites
There are a number of official camping grounds around Lake Como and Lake Lugano. Among the better ones are **Lido** at Menaggio (tel: 0344 31150, open May–Sep), and **Serenella** at Gravedona (tel: 0334 89452, open Apr–Sep).

WHERE TO EAT

Many of the so-called best restaurants are in the large hotels, but their food tends to be international. Plenty of restaurants serve local specialities, including fish from the lake. For budget eating try local trattorias and pizzerias.

LUXURY
Locanda del Boschetta, via Boschetta 8, Lugano, Switzerland, tel: (41) 91 542 493. One of Lugano's best restaurants, noted for its Ticino specialities.
Bilacus, salita Serbelloni 9, Bellagio, tel: 031 950 263. Often claimed to be Bellagio's best restaurant. Beautiful terrace for alfresco eating.
Imbacadero, piazza Cavour 20, Como, tel: 031 270 166. Hotel restaurant with tables on the square and local cuisine.
Vecchia Varenna, via Scoscesa 10, Varenna, tel:

0341 830 793. Summer eating on terrace facing the lake. Local specialities. Closed Mon.

MID-RANGE
Trattoria del Gino, via Camozzi 16, Menaggio. Simple local dishes and a good tourist menu.
Restaurante Teatro Socialle, via Maestri Comocini, Como, tel: 031 264 042. Reasonably priced menu in this theatre restaurant near the cathedral.
Silvio, via Carcano 12, Bellagio, tel: 031 950 322. Specializes in local dishes, particularly lake fish.

BUDGET
La Scuderia, piazza Matteotti 4, Como. Cheap pizzeria near bus station. Closed Thursday.
Le Colonne, Piazza Mazzini, Como, tel: 031 266 166. Good value, close to the lake shore.
La Grotta, salita Cernaia 14, Bellagio. Excellent for cheap, tasty pizzas. Closed Monday.
Ostello La Primula, via IV Novembre 38, Menaggio. You do not have to be a hosteller to use the superb value restaurant of this youth hostel.

SHOPPING

The best shopping centre around Lake Como is undoubtedly the city of **Como**, where good bargains can be had in leather goods, fashion clothing, watches and jewellery. **Lugano** also has some fashionable shops, although prices are more

expensive than in Italy. Chocolates and leather goods are particularly noteworthy.

TOURS AND EXCURSIONS

The vast majority of the tour destinations are on the lake shore, so that many of the places can be reached independently by using service boats. The most popular site is **Villa Carlotta**. Other commonly visited places include **Isola Comacina** and the villages of **Bellagio** and **Varenna**. On Lake Lugano, the main excursion venue is the attractive little village of **Marcote**.

USEFUL CONTACTS

Tourist Information Offices: **Como**, Piazza Cavour. Open 09:00–13:00 and 14:30–18:00 Mon–Sat Oct–May, 09:30–12:30 Sun; same hours Mon–Sat Jun–Sep, 14:30–18:00 Sun; tel: 031 269 712; website: www.lakecomo.com
Cernobbio, largo L. Visconti 4, tel: 031 510 198.
Menaggio, piazza Garibaldi 8, tel: 0344 32924.
Varenna, Piazza San Giorgio, tel: 0341 830 3677.
Bellagio, Piazza della Chiesa, tel: 031 950 204.
Lecco, Via N. Sauro, off Piazza Garibaldi, tel: 0341 362 360.
Lugano, Palazzo Civico (Town Hall), Riva Albertolli, tel: (41) 91 921 4664, website: www.tourism-ticino.ch
Lake Transport Information: Lake Lugano, tel: 091 971 5223. Lake Como, tel: 031 579 211.

6
Lake Garda
and Verona

Garda is the largest of the northern Italian lakes and, indeed, the largest lake in Italy, measuring 50km (31 miles) from north to south. Scenically, Lake Garda presents contrasts. The north of the lake is narrow, steep-sided and fiord-like, while the south of the lake is wider, with rolling hills forming the shoreline. A glacier was responsible for scouring out the lake and also for depositing low hills of moraine in the south. Weather-wise, Garda is milder than the other lakes, with the south having what borders on a Mediterranean climate, enabling citrus fruit, olives and vines to grow in profusion. Spectacular thunderstorms can occur in late summer, particularly in the mountainous north of the lake. Strong winds in the afternoon, especially around Tarbole, make this area one of the world's prime wind-surfing locations.

The shores of Lake Garda are also full of historical interest. The area of prehistoric rock engravings near the Punta San Vigilio provides the earliest evidence of human occupation. Lake Garda also has more Roman remains than any other part of northern Italy, with important villas at Sirmione and Desenzano. Later the Scaligeri dynasty of Verona built a number of castles around the lake shore. There are particularly fine examples at Sirmione and Malcésine.

Today, Lake Garda is the most popular of the northern Italian lakes and is the most orientated towards tourism. The lake is particularly attractive to German and Austrian visitors, who pour over the Alps in their

DON'T MISS

*** Gardaland: outstanding theme park near Peschiera.
*** The Roman Arena: at Verona; once the haunt of gladiators, now the unusual venue for summer operas.
** Scaligeri castles: distinctive lakeside castles at Sirmione, Malcésine and Riva.
** Il Vittoriale: house and gardens of poet and eccentric Gabriele d'Annunzio.
* Piramidi di Zone: curious geological formations in the form of earth pinnacles topped with boulders.

Opposite: *An exciting roller coaster ride at the Gardaland Theme Park.*

LAKE GARDA'S CLIMATE

The **winter** climate of Garda
is milder than that of the
other lakes, at around 6°C
(43°F). It also has warmer
summer weather, so that
the southern part of the
lake in particular has a
semi-Mediterranean climate.
Rainfall is light but the
northern part of the lake has
some spectacular thunder-
storms in the late summer.
The best months weather-
wise for touring are May,
June and September.

thousands. During the summer months, the water can
be congested with boats and the roads can be blocked
with vehicles. There are a number of **golf courses**
around the southern shores of the lake and it is here that
we find several **theme parks**. **Gardaland**, the area's
answer to Disneyland, is a particular favourite with
children, while there are no fewer than three aquaparks.
Yet, despite this popularity, Lake Garda is certainly not
spoiled. It has a longer tourist season than the other
lakes and even in the winter it can be a most attractive
place to take a holiday.

LAKE GARDA'S WESTERN SHORE

The **Gardesana Occidentale** or western shore of Lake
Garda forms one of the most spectacular drives in Italy.
Initially the scenery is fairly tame and gives no indication
of the delights to come. The rolling hills form a region
known as the **Valtenisi**, with a few old villages such as
Padenghe, **San Felice** and **Moniga**, the latter with a
delightful little port and castle. Near **Manerba** a rocky
headland capped by a ruined *rocca* protrudes into the
lake. The fortress looks out over the water towards **Isola
di Garda**, the largest island on the lake. The island once
had a monastery, but this fell into ruins and the island is
now the home of a magnificent private villa.

Below: *Lake Garda has
many attractive lakeside
resorts with opportunities
for water sports.*

Salò

It is unfortunate, perhaps,
that Salò's main claim to
fame is that it was the
headquarters of Mussolini's
puppet republic set up
by the Germans towards
the end of World War II.
Today Salò is an attractive
town located on a wide
bay fringed by a delightful
promenade. It has a 15th-
century Gothic **Cathedral**
and although the interior

LAKE GARDA FACTS

Lake Garda is the largest of the northern Italian lakes and the biggest lake in Italy.
Area: 370km² (145 sq miles).
Length: 50km (31 miles).
Maximum width: 16km (10 miles).
Average depth: 135m (445ft).

Left: *The lakeside resort of Salò was the headquarters of Mussolini's puppet government towards the end of World War II.*

is rather gloomy, there are some fine paintings to admire, including a *Madonna and Saints* by Romanino. There are two museums of interest. Attached to the town hall is the **Museo Civico Archeologico**, with artefacts from the local area. The **Museo del Nastro Azzuro** (the Blue Ribbon Museum) in Via Fantoni is dedicated to prominent Italian military figures and their weapons and uniforms from the period 1797–1945. Open all year, 16:00–18:00 Saturday, 10:00–12:30 and 17:00–19:00 Sunday.

The scenery dramatically improves north of Salò, where the **Gardone Riviera** claims to have the best climate in the whole of the Italian lake area. Benefiting from the mild winters are parks and public gardens, particularly the **Giardino Botanico Hruska**, which displays over 8000 plants varying in origin from Alpine to Mediterranean. (Open 09:00–12:00 and 14:00–18:00 from March to October).

Il Vittoriale **

On the hillside above Gardone is the villa known as Il Vittoriale (The Victory), the former home of **Gabriele d'Annunzio**, the poet and eccentric. He was given the villa by Mussolini in 1925 and d'Annunzio turned it into an extraordinary museum that illustrates the bizarre nature of the man. The house is kept in the semidarkness that d'Annunzio preferred. As well as a library of

GOLF IN THE LAKES AREA

Golf is a sport that is rapidly increasing in popularity in northern Italy. There are now nearly 30 courses within a 40km (25-mile) radius of Milan. The larger lakes have golf courses around their shores, usually in the lower-lying land to the south. Lake Garda, for example, has five courses, three of 27 holes, one of 18 holes and one of nine holes. There are eight around Lake Maggiore and a few around Lake Como. Many clubs are encouraging foreign players to take a golf and holiday package.

Above: *The resort of Limone is backed by terraces of lemon trees and vines.*

priceless books, the tour reveals such macabre items as the coffin that the poet used to lie in to meditate, and his pet tortoise embalmed in bronze after it had died from overeating. The gardens are also full of interest, with an open-air theatre and d'Annunzio's mausoleum.

The writer's coffin is flanked by those of his followers and war comrades. Nearby is the World War I warship, the *Puglia*, which was hauled up the hillside to its final resting place. Also on display is the aircraft from which d'Annunzio dropped propaganda leaflets over Vienna, and two of the cars that the poet drove flamboyantly into battle. Not surprisingly, this bizarre place is one of Lake Garda's major attractions. Potential visitors should be aware that Il Vittoriale is so popular that at peak periods numbers may be restricted and it is necessary to arrive well before the opening time to be sure of getting a ticket. Open daily 08:30–20:00 April–September, 09:00– 17:00 October–March.

Toscolano-Maderno

The next town on the western shore is **Toscolano-Maderno**, an amalgamation of two villages built partially on the alluvial fan built up by the River Toscolano. This was the largest town on Lake Garda during Roman times and a 1st-century villa has been discovered here with some well-preserved mosaics. Toscolano had a famous printing press in the 15th century, and paper-making is still an important industry in the area. The elegant Romanesque **Church of Sant' Andrea** is worth a look for its paintings by Paolo Veneziano. Take a glance at the tourist office, which has two cannonballs embedded in its walls, relics of the naval bombardment by the Austrians in 1866. On the north side of the town is **Villa Feltrinelli**, the home of Mussolini during the short-lived Salò Republic. Lake Garda's only car ferry runs from Toscolano-Maderno to Torri del Bernaco on the eastern shore.

LEMON GROWING

The town of **Limone** may have got its name from the lemons that once grew here. Lemons were introduced to the area by monks in the 13th century, but growing these and other citrus fruit was difficult because the crop is ruined if the temperature drops below -3°C. The trees, supported by pillars and sometimes covered with glass, were grown on terraced south-facing slopes. Stoves were lit if frost threatened. Lemon cultivation declined after the unification of Italy, as cheap lemons were available from frost-free Sicily, and today only a few lemon groves are found around Lake Garda.

Gargnano

Gargnano, surrounded by old citrus terraces, is well known as a sailing centre. It is also the site of a 13th-century Franciscan monastery with some well-preserved cloisters. A popular excursion from Gargnano is inland via a tortuous mountain road to the Val Toscanino and Lake Valvestino, which has been dammed to provide hydroelectric power. The road continues, winding its way down to Lake Idro.

Limone sul Garda

After Gargnano the lake shore becomes steep and the road frequently tunnels into the mountains. The last notable town on the western shore is **Limone sul Garda**, a former fishing village which has expanded into a thriving resort that many consider has been ruined by tourism. Old citrus terraces with their concrete supporting posts line the hillside. Limone was the first place in Europe to grow lemons, but today many of the terraces have been converted into vineyards. There is a historic quarter behind the fishing port with a couple of interesting churches, but the ambience is overwhelmed by the stalls and shops selling cheap souvenirs.

Riva del Garda

Located at the northern tip of the lake, Riva has always been of strategic importance, being held at various times by Verona, Milan, Venice, the French and the Austrians. During the Austrian rule from 1813–1918 it became a popular resort and was described as the 'Southern Pearl on the Austro-Hungarian Riviera'. It continues, today, to be the most stylish resort on Lake Garda and attracts many German and Austrian tourists. Next to the shore is the moated **castle**, built in the 12th century by the Scaligeri to defend the town against waterborne pirates. The castle now houses the **Museo Civico**, which displays paintings, sculpture and finds from the

> **GABRIELE D'ANNUNZIO**
> **(1863–1938)**
>
> Born Gaetano Rapgnetta in a humble family, he changed his name to Gabriel of the Annunciation. Initially the greatest poet and novelist of his generation, d'Annunzio achieved greater fame as an eccentric soldier and socialite, having scandalous affairs with many women. He was an ardent right-wing nation-alist and he campaigned fervently for Italy to enter World War I, in which he lost an eye in combat. At the conclusion of the war he gathered together a band of men and marched on Fiume, which he considered should have been given to Italy. D'Annunzio ruled the city for a year before being forced to abdicate. Mussolini, who regarded him as an embar-rassment, gave him, in compensation, a villa on Lake Garda, where d'Annunzio spent the rest of his life in a world of total exhibitionism.

Below: *Riva is the most stylish resort on Lake Garda and is popular with German visitors.*

GALLEONS ON LAKE GARDA

The size of Lake Garda has lent itself to waterborne battles, and none was more bizarre than the naval skirmish between Milan and the Venetians in the 13th century. Venice decided to bring a fleet of 26 ships overland to the town of Torbole at the north of the lake. The boats were hauled overland by ox carts and then rowed up the Adige River to Lago di Lappio. There they were dismantled and carted over the pass to Torbole – a journey that had taken three months. They were rebuilt, but were barely seaworthy, so it was hardly surprising that the fleet was defeated by the Milanese.

Bronze-Age settlement at nearby Lake Ledro (*see* below). The museum is open 09:30–18:30 Tuesday–Sunday, 09:30–22:30 July and August. The castle butts on to Riva's main square, the Piazza III Novembre. Dominating the square is the 13th-century clock tower, the **Torre Apponale**, which can be entered using the museum ticket. Outstanding among the buildings in the main square are the **Palazzo Pretorio**, built in 1376, and the 15th-century **Palazzo Communale**. Among the churches in Riva, the best is undoubtedly the **Inviolata**, which was built in 1603 and has a number of fine frescoes and paintings. In Piazza Garibaldi is a museum you will either love or hate. This is **Reptiland**, which has a comprehensive collection of creepy crawlies including snakes, tarantulas, giant beetles and scorpions. Open daily 11:00–20:00, April–October.

The area around Riva is rich in interest. The large pipe on the mountainside behind the town is part of a hydro-electric scheme using water from Lake Ledro. More waterworks, this time of a natural kind, can be seen near the village of Tenno, where a waterfall, known as the **Cascata del Varonne**, crashes down 87m (287ft) in a dark, spray-filled gorge. An interesting excursion can be made by taking the mountain road west to **Lake Ledro**. The eastern end of the lake was the site of Bronze-Age pile dwellings, and many of the stakes can be seen when the demands of Riva's hydroelectric scheme lowers the level of water in the lake. One of the dwellings has been reconstructed near the village of **Molina di Ledro** at the eastern end of the lake, where the **Museo delle Palafitte** displays jewellery, pottery and weapons found at the site. Opening times vary according to the season. The road continues past the lake and the small resort of **Pieve de Ledro** and through the gorge of Valle d'Ampola before dropping down to Lake Idro.

Below: *Italian ice cream is widely acknowledged to be the best in the world.*

LAKE GARDA'S EASTERN SHORE

The **Gardesana Orientale** or Garda's eastern shore is entirely within the province of Verona. The shoreline is lower than the west side of the lake, but backed by the limestone massif of **Monte Baldo**, which rises to 2130m (6989ft). The eastern shore is often called the **Olive Riviera**, on account of the large number of olive groves to be seen.

Torbole

Only a few kilometres separates Riva from Torbole, a popular wind-surfing resort. The Sarca River, which is the main feeder of Lake Garda, runs through the town and provides the pass

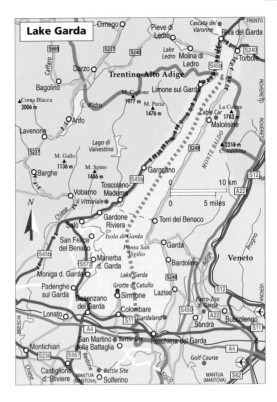

whereby the N240 runs east to the Adige Valley. Torbole is above all a young persons' resort, with the emphasis on outdoor activities of many kinds. The streets are full of roller bladers, joggers and mountain bikers – all in their specialist kits.

Further south is the beautifully situated town of **Malcésine**, distinguished by its 13th-century **Scaligeri castle**, which seems to rise directly out of the waters of the lake. With its tulip-like crenellations and battlements the castle is truly distinctive. Inside is a **museum** with natural history and archaeological sections. One room is devoted to the German writer, Goethe, who was briefly imprisoned here, being suspected of spying after he was seen sketching the lake! The old part of

LAKE GARDA'S MARKETS

One of the delights of taking a holiday in the Lake Garda region is to visit the weekly street markets on the following days:
Monday: Peschiera, Torri del Benaco.
Tuesday: Desenzano, Limone, Torbole.
Wednesday: Gargnano, Riva.
Thursday: Bardolino.
Friday: Garda, Sirmione.
Saturday: Malcésine, Salò.
Sunday: Bardolino.

Above: *Torri del Benaco is a charming little resort halfway down the eastern shore of Lake Garda.*

Malcésine is a maze of narrow streets backing the charming little harbour. The only building of real note is the **Palazzo dei Capitani del Lago**. Dating from the 15th century, it is now the town hall.

A wonderful excursion from Malcésine is by cable car to **Monte Baldo**. The journey takes 30 minutes and the top station is at 1650m (5410ft). From here there are a number of hiking trails, including one along the main ridge to the summit. The mountain is noted for its rare plants and it is a popular ski resort in the winter.

Torri del Benaco

Further south is Torri del Benaco, arguably the most attractive and least spoiled of Garda's lakeside villages. From here a car ferry crosses the lake to Maderno. Torri also has a **Scaligeri castle**. It dates from 1383 and is now a **museum** which has displays on the trades of the area such as the production of olive oil, wine, citrus fruits and fishing. South of Torri is the headland of **Punta San Vigilio**, with a little church of the same name. There are stunning views in all directions.

Garda

Sandwiched between the headlands of Punta San Vigilio and Rocca del Garda is the town of **Garda**. The name comes from the German *warten* or fortress, referring to the walls of the town, although few of these remain. Set back from the small port is an attractive tree-lined promenade, where a market is held on Fridays. Among the cobbled alleyways is the **Church of Santa Maria Maggiore**. Although the church dates largely from the 18th century, there is a well-preserved 15th-century cloister.

THE WORK OF GIANTS?

Just north of Torbole is the village of **Nago**, where there are some huge potholes near the old river bed. These are known as the **Marmitte dei Giganti** or the 'Pots of the Giants'. Some of these potholes are several metres across, but their origin had nothing to do with giants. We have to go back to the Ice Age, some 15,000 years ago, when torrents of glacial meltwater were pouring down from the Alps. Huge boulders were carried in the torrents and were swirled around on the bed of the river, wearing out the potholes by abrasion.

Bardolino

To the south of Garda is **Bardolino**, the centre of an area famous for the production of wine and olive oil. There are museums dedicated to both of these liquids. The **Museo del Vino**, at via Costabella 9, shows the methods of production and offers wine tasting. (Open daily 09:00–13:00 and 14:00–18:00, March–October.) The **Museo dell'Olio d'Oliva** can be found at via Peschiera 54. (Open 09:00–12:30 and 15:00–19:00, closed on Sunday and Wednesday afternoon.) Bardolino is at its most lively during the *Fiesta del Uva*, the Festival of the Grape, which is held between mid-September and mid-October.

Bardolino has a number of churches, the most interesting of which are the 11th-century Romanesque **San Severo** with some good frescoes and an imposing campanile, and the 8th-century **San Zeno** with its cruciform structure and curious semicircular apses.

Lazise

The last town on the eastern shore is **Lazise**, with remains of the town walls and yet another Scaligeri castle. There has been a port here since the Venetian occupation and it is said that in those days a chain could be drawn from the castle across the harbour entrance. Next to the quay is the 12th-century **Church of San Niccolò**, with some highly regarded frescoes, and the arcaded medieval former **customs house**. Just outside Lazise is **Gardaland**, one of the largest theme parks in Italy. If you have bored children, this might be just the place to go (*see* page 13).

LAKE GARDA'S SOUTHERN SHORE

The southern shore of Lake Garda is low lying with a few rolling hills of glacial moraine. The towns of **Peschiera** and **Desenzano**

OLIVE OIL

So many olive trees are grown on the southeast shores of Lake Garda that this has become known as the 'Olive Riviera'. The olive harvest begins around mid-November and continues until January. The milling of the olives is nowadays an industrial process. The quality of the oil depends on its acidity – the best oil has less than one per cent. This is known as 'Extra Virgin', which is green in colour. What better memento of a holiday in the Lake Garda area than a bottle of high-quality extra virgin olive oil? What's more, it contains no cholesterol and is an essential part of a healthy Mediterranean diet.

Below: *Bardolino has two excellent museums and a lively grape festival.*

THE FOUNDING OF THE RED CROSS

Perhaps the only good thing about the slaughter of thousands of soldiers at the battles of Solfarino and San Martino della Battaglia was the founding of the Red Cross organization. A Swiss gentleman, **Henry Dunant** from Geneva, was in the area trying to present a petition to Napoleon III. Dunant was appalled by the carnage of the battles and he helped local villagers to care for the wounded. On his return to Geneva, he wrote a book describing the battles and the large number of injured. Within two years the International Committee of the Red Cross was formed. Later Dunant was awarded the first **Nobel Peace Prize**, but sadly he became bankrupt and spent the last years of his life in a home for impoverished men.

make good bases for visiting the lake. Between them is the remarkable town of **Sirmione**, which should be on every visitor's itinerary.

Peschiera del Garda

Located where the River Mincio drains Lake Garda, Peschiera has been a strategic town throughout its history. The Romans built the town's first defensive walls, which were extended and strengthened, first by the Scaligeri of Verona and later by the Venetians. Finally the Austrians, two centuries later, added two more towers. Today, it is possible to walk along part of the walls giving views over the town and the sizeable fishing harbour. There is not too much to see in the town itself apart from the 18th-century **Church of San Martino**, which has some impressive frescoes. The town hall clock in the main square is also of interest – two bronze eagles strike the bell with their beaks on the hour.

Sirmione

Positioned on a low 4km (2.5-mile) long peninsula, Sirmione has one of the most spectacular sites in Italy. The medieval core of the town occupies the rocky tip of the peninsula, protected by the **Rocca Scaligeri** built by the Verona dynasty in the 13th century. Surrounded by a moat full of wildfowl and approached over a drawbridge, the castle is an imposing sight. Although there is not much to

see inside the fortress, it is worth climbing up to the crenellated, tulip-shaped battlements and towers for a wonderful view over the roofs of the town to the point of the peninsula and the lake beyond. Next to the castle is the **Church of Santa Maria Maggiore**, with the usual set of frescoes. Note, too, the Roman capital that has been set into the façade. Next to the church is the start of the *passegiatta panoramica* that runs along to the northern point of the peninsula.

Few tourists find their way to the end of the peninsula, but it is full of interest. There has been a spa here since Roman times, making use of the hot sulphurous water that originates beneath the lake bed. There is a large excavation site here, known as the **Grotte di Catullo**, named after the Roman poet Catullus. It was once thought that this was his villa, but such is the size of the area covered it can only have been a Roman spa. A small **museum** displays some of the artefacts and mosaics that have been recovered. The Grotte and the museum are open 08:30–19:00 Tuesday–Saturday, 09:00–18:00 Sunday from March to October; 08:30–16:30 Tuesday–Saturday, 09:00–16:30 Sunday from November to February. Nearby, occupying the highest point of the tip of the peninsula, is the **Church of San Pietro**. Romanesque in style, it was founded in the 8th century and has a good collection of frescoes dating from the 13th to the 16th centuries.

The old town of Sirmione is usually heaving with people, many of whom arrive by boat. Fortunately, traffic is not allowed past the castle. If arriving by car you will have to park and walk over the drawbridge.

Desenzano del Garda

At the southwest corner of the lake, Desenzano is the Lake Garda's largest town. As a transport centre, it is a good starting point for visiting the lake – close to the A4 *autostrada* and on the main railway line from Milan to Venice. Many of the lake steamers call at the attractive little harbour. There are one or two items of interest in

Above: *The town of Sirmione is protected by the Rocca Scaligeri.*
Opposite: *One of the many rides at the Gardaland Theme Park.*

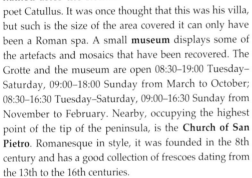

GARDALAND

The main attraction for children in the Lake Garda region is Gardaland, Italy's answer to Disneyland. Situated just to the north of Peschiera, it opened in 1975 and covers over 500,000m^2 (60,000 sq yd). There are 38 attractions, including an exciting roller coaster, a dolphin pool, Jungle Rapids, a Cinema Dinamico, a simulation of the Valley of the Kings, and a Blue Tornado that gives the opportunity to take the controls of the American fighter plane – ideal for a family day out!

Above: *Piazza Brà is the focal point of life in the city of Verona.*

the town, including the Baroque **Church of Santa Maria Magdalena**, well known for Tiepolo's unusual version of the *Last Supper*. It features serving women and a dog, as well as the Apostles. Also worth a visit is the **Roman Villa** in Via Crocifisso. Dating from the 3rd century and excavated in 1921, it was obviously owned by a wealthy family and has some mosaics in excellent condition. Open 08:30–19:00 Tuesday–Saturday, March to October; 08:30–16:30 Tuesday–Saturday, November to February.

Notorious Battles

The plain south of Desenzano has been fought over by armies throughout history, but during the fight for Italian independence there occurred here, on the same day, two of the bloodiest battles ever. On 24 June 1859 at **San Martino della Battaglia**, Victor Emmanuel II and his Sardinian army defeated the Austrian right wing, while 11km (7 miles) to the southwest Napoleon III annihilated the main army of Emperor Franz Joseph at **Solferino**. Casualties were huge. At San Martino, a chapel contains the bones of over 2600 dead from both sides, while at Solferino over 7000 French and Austrian troops are buried. Both towns have museums and monuments to remember the dead.

LAKE ISEO FACTS

Lake Iseo is the fifth largest of the northern Italian lakes.
Length: 24km (15 miles).
Maximum width: 5km (3 miles).
Maximum depth: 250m (820ft).
Lake Iseo also has the largest island of any lake in Europe in Monte Isola.

LAKE ISEO

Lying midway between lakes Como and Garda and situated just to the northwest of the town of Brescia, Lake Iseo is the fifth largest of the northern Italian lakes. It is, however, the least known outside Italy, although very popular with Italians. In the north of the lake around the town of **Lovere** are steep cliffs falling directly into the lake, giving it a fiord-like appearance. In the south the main town is the transport centre of **Iseo**.

Nearby is the village of **Zone**, which has some remarkable erosion features called the **Pyramidi di Zone**. These soft glacial deposits, known as erosion pyramids, have been worn away by erosion, leaving behind thin pillars topped by granite boulders.

Towards the southern end of Lake Iseo is **Monte Isola**, the largest island in the Italian lakes. This island is essentially a huge mountain rising some 400m (1312ft) above the surface of the lake. It is capped by the **Church of the Madonna della Ceriola**, which is an important place of pilgrimage.

At the southern end of Lake Iseo is a large wetland area called the **Torbiere**, protected because of its wildlife and the remains of prehistoric pile dwellings.

> ### SCALIGERI NICKNAMES
>
> The Scaligeri dynasty were ruthless rulers of Verona and the Lake Garda area during the 13th and 14th centuries. The founder of the dynasty was **Mastino I**. Mastino means 'mastiff' and as a mark of respect all other male members of the family had some mention of dogs in their names. After **Mastino II**, all the male rulers had the prefix 'can' or dog added to their name. **Cangrande**, for example, was 'big dog' and **Cansignorio** was 'top dog'. Less endearing, however, was **Canrabbiaso** or 'mad dog'.

VERONA

Most visitors to Lake Garda will probably land at Verona Airport and it is well worth spending a day or two in this ancient city before going on to the lake area. Verona is situated on a meander of the **River Adige**. This was a good defensive position to guard the routes coming south from the Alps and east–west across the Plain of Lombardy. Verona was an important Roman city

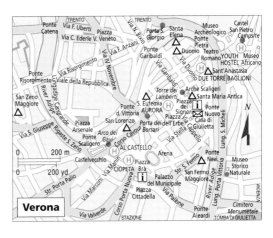

Verona

WHEREFORE ART THOU ROMEO?

During the 12th and 13th centuries in Verona there was an ongoing feud between the Cappelletti and Montechi families. The 16th-century Italian writer **Luigi da Porta** wrote a story based on this feud, which was adapted by Shakespeare, who changed the names to Capulet and Montague in his play ***Romeo and Juliet***. A number of sites in Verona are associated with the play, such as Juliet's house, Romeo's house and Juliet's grave. Although the connections are dubious, this does not appear to worry tourists, who are happy to soak up the associations, particularly at the balcony of Juliet's house.

---

a number of remains from this period have survived. Later it was an important city-state, typified by feuds amongst powerful local families. During the 13th and 14th centuries Verona came under the rule of the Scaligeri dynasty. Although fiercely authoritarian, they were also great benefactors of the arts. Verona was then briefly under the control of the Viscontis before having four centuries of Venetian rule. On the collapse of the Venetian Empire, Verona came successively under the rule of the French and the Austrians, before the unification of Italy.

Verona's Main Sights

The focal point of life in Verona is the elegant **Piazza Brà**, which is dominated by the immense **Roman Arena**. Built in the 1st century AD, it has an oval ground plan measuring 152m (498ft) by 123m (403 ft). An earthquake in the 12th century destroyed much of the outer wall – that which remains is known as the wing. Over 20,000 spectators were able to watch gladiatorial contests, but today they flood in to watch the **opera festival** that takes place here during July and August. The Arena is open from 08:00–19:00 Tuesday–Sunday, and during opera season from 08:15–15:30 Tuesday–Sunday.

Below: *The Roman arena, site of Verona's famous summer opera festival.*

Northeast of the Arena is the **Piazza dell'Erbe**, home of an ancient market selling vegetables and herbs. The market stalls remain today, but mostly sell tourist souvenirs and fast food. In the centre of the square almost concealed by the stalls is an old Roman fountain, while around the edge of the square are numerous fine houses and palaces. The Piazza dell'Erbe almost merges with the much quieter **Piazza dei Signori**. Good views of both squares and the rest of the town can be seen from the top of the **Torre dei Lamberti**, which fortunately has a lift. In front of the Romanesque **Church of Santa Maria Antica** are the **Arche Scaligeri**, the tombs of the Scaligeri family. Most imperious of all is the equestrian statue of Cangrande I, while the other tombs have elaborate wrought-iron grilles.

Above: *The balcony where Shakespeare's Romeo and Juliet are supposed to have courted.*

A couple of blocks away from Piazza dell'Erbe, in Via Capello, is the **Casa di Giulietta** – Juliet's House. This is the Juliet of Shakespeare's *Romeo and Juliet* fame, and although the characters are largely fictional this does not deter the thousands of visitors that flock here annually to be photographed on the balcony. The 14th-century house is attractive enough, but a suitor would have to be extremely athletic to climb up to the balcony. 'Romeo's House' is situated close by and 'Juliet's Grave' is an empty sarcophagus in a nearby monastery. Open 08:00–19:00, closed on Mondays.

The Castelvecchio Area

There is another collection of monuments to the south-west of the historic core of Verona. The **Porta dei Borsari** used to be the city's largest Roman gate and probably dates from the 1st century. The **Castelvecchio** (old castle), with a superb riverside position, was built by the Scaligeri in the mid-14th century and it formed their main stronghold. In later times it was a college, and the French and Austrians used it as a barracks. It was badly

---

OPERA AT THE ARENA

The opera festival at Verona runs through July and August and usually features many of the favourite Italian operas performed by world-famous singers. A visit to the Verona opera ought to be on everyone's itinerary, but a few words of advice are helpful. Remember that this is a Roman arena and the seats are extremely hard, so hire a cushion or bring one of your own. Seats are very expensive, but cheaper if bought on the day. Performances start at 21:00, when every member of the audience lights a small candle, giving the whole arena a marvellous atmosphere. However, opera-goers should be prepared for poor acoustics, noisy children and less than adequate toilets.

Above: *Verona's Ponte Scaligero, with the Castelvecchio to the left of the bridge.*

damaged in World War II, but has been fully restored and today houses the town **museum**. It has a fascinating collection of paintings, sculpture, jewellery and weapons. It is open from 08:00–19:00, closed on Mondays. Next to the Castelvecchio is a Roman Triumphal Arch, the **Arco dei Gavi**. It was destroyed by Napoleon's troops, but rebuilt in the 1930s. On the other side of the castle, spanning the River Adige, is the **Ponte Scaligero**, a bridge built by Cangrande II in the 14th century. It was blown up by the retreating Germans in 1945, but this too has been faithfully restored from the debris.

Northeast of the River

The Roman **Ponte Pietra** crosses the Adige to a group of monuments, museums and churches in the northeast of the town. The most important is the **Teatro Romano**, a Roman theatre dating back to the first century and probably older than the Arena. It is an amphitheatre with semicircular seating and it is used in the summer months for plays and concerts. At the back of the theatre is a lift that takes visitors up to the **Museo Archeologico**, which is based in an old convent. Both the theatre and the museum are open 09:00–15:00 Tuesday–Sunday, July and August; 09:00–18:30 September–June. There are two other mildly interesting museums on this side of the river – the **Museo Storico Naturale** at lungadige Porta Victoria 9, open 09:00–19:00 Monday–Saturday, and the **Museo Africano**, at vicolo Pozzo 1, open 09:00–12:00 and 15:00–18:00 Tuesday–Saturday.

NORTHERN ITALY'S MOTORWAYS

For the tourist motoring east–west across the Plain of Lombardy there is no need to experience the traffic snarl-ups in Verona, because the excellent *autostrada* bypasses the city. The *autostrada* system centres on Milan, making it easy to reach all parts of the region. The speed limit is 130kph (75mph), although this may be lowered during holiday periods. Remember, however, that the *autostradas* are toll roads and charges can mount up surprisingly quickly.

Verona's Churches

Verona has a wealth of interesting churches. Located at the most northerly bend of the river is the red and white striped **Duomo** or cathedral. It has a wonderful façade with elegantly carved portals. The lower part of the building is Romanesque, merging into Gothic at higher levels. The interior has some beautiful carving in the chapels. Look particularly in the first chapel on the left, where the altarpiece contains Titian's *Assumption*. More impressive than the Duomo, however, is the **Church of San Zeno Maggiore**, which is located just over a kilometre northwest of the Castelvecchio. It dates from the first half of the 12th century and has been described as the most significant Romanesque church in northern Italy. Of particular importance are the large rose window, the 48 relief panels on the bronze doors, and the triptych by Andrea Mantegna. San Zeno also has an imposing campanile and some elegant arcaded cloisters. Close to the Plaza dei Signori is the massive Gothic **Church of Sant'Anastasia**, Verona's largest church. Although rather plain on the outside, the interior is more interesting. Look for the fresco of *St George and the Princess* to the right of the main altar.

Other churches of note are **San Lorenzo**, near the Castelvecchio, which has an unusual women's gallery, and the 9th-century **Santa Elena** adjacent to the Duomo. It is possible to obtain a pass that allows admission to all the churches in Verona that belong to the *Chiese Vive* (Living Churches group). Better still is the **Verona Card**, which, for a remarkably cheap fee, gives admission to all the city's churches, museums and buses over a three-day period. Remember, however, that all the museums close on a Monday.

THE SHAKESPEARE CONNECTION

William Shakespeare, generally acknowledged to be the world's greatest playwright, wrote a number of dramas with northern Italian connections. His *Romeo and Juliet*, a love affair based on two feuding families in Verona, is well known, as is the *Merchant of Venice*. Less frequently performed is *The Two Gentlemen of Verona*, a comedy involving businessmen, their families and their love affairs. Surprisingly, there is no evidence that Shakespeare ever visited Italy.

Below: *San Zeno Maggiore – this basilica is claimed to be the most beautiful Romanesque church in northern Italy.*

Lake Garda and Verona at a Glance

BEST TIMES TO VISIT

Many attractions around Lake Garda close in winter, while the summer months of July and August can be extremely crowded and hot. Unless you are an opera fan, avoid Verona in August when hotels will be fully booked. **Spring** is undoubtedly the most pleasant season to visit Lake Garda, as the gardens will be in full flower and the higher mountains will still have a capping of snow. September and October, when the crowds have gone home, can also be an enjoyable time to visit.

GETTING THERE

The most convenient airport is Verona, just a 20-minute drive from the lake. The area is also well served by *autostradas*, with the A22 following the Adige valley from the Alps and the A4 running east–west along the Lombardy Plain to the south. **Railways** closely follow the *autostrada* routes, with the Milan–Venice line calling at Verona, Peschiera and Desenzano.

GETTING AROUND

Visitors with a **car** will find that it is perfectly possible to drive right around Lake Garda in a day, although few would want to tour at this speed. A more leisurely way of seeing the lake is by **boat**, and a variety of craft are available, from speedy hydrofoils to traditional lake steamers. Most

monuments, churches and museums can be reached on foot.

WHERE TO STAY

There is a wide variety of accommodation available both around Lake Garda and in Verona. Many lakeside hotels, however, may be fully booked. It is essential to book ahead during the height of summer and especially in Verona during the opera season in July and August.

LUXURY

Grand Hotel Fasano, via Zanardelli 160, Gardone Riviera, tel: 0365 290 220, fax: 0365 290 221. An 18th-century Habsburg hunting lodge converted into a hotel in 1900. In lakeside park with wide range of sports facilities.
Du Lac et du Parc, viale Rovereto 44, Riva del Garda, tel: 0464 551 500, fax: 0464 555 200. Lakeside hotel in large park. Well-appointed rooms. Closed Nov–Mar.
Palace Hotel, via Grotte 6, Sirmione, tel: 030 990 5890, fax: 030 916 390. Neo-classical villa with subtropical gardens and elegant rooms.
Due Torre Baglioni, piazza Sant'Anastasia 4, Verona, tel: 045 595 044. High-class traditional hotel in the historic core of the city.

MID-RANGE

Guilietta e Romeo, Vicolo Tre Marchetti, Verona, tel:

045 800 3554. Small, friendly hotel just off the Piazza Brà.
Flora, via Giorgione 27, Garda, tel: 045 725 5008. On higher ground above the town, with gardens and pools.
Vega, Viale Roma, Malcésine, tel: 045 657 0355 fax: 045 740 1604. Modern hotel, well-equipped rooms; private beach.
Il Valiero, Via T. da Molin, Desenzano del Garda, tel: 030 914 1318 fax: 030 914 0322. Has its own beach close to the boat terminals.

BUDGET

Diana, lungolago d'Annunzio 30, Gardone Riviera, tel: 0365 21815. Simple rooms at small lakeside hotel.
Mercedes, via Nanzello 12, Limone, tel: 0365 954 073. Bargain rates, pool and views.
Catullo, via Priori 11, Malcésine, tel: 045 740 0352. Good value small hotel with a swimming pool.
Giardinetto, Via V. Bellini, Riva del Garda, tel: 045 725 5051, fax: 045 627 8302. Comfortable small hotel. All rooms have lake views.

Youth Hostels

Lake Garda's only youth hostel is at **Riva**, piazza Cavour 10, tel: 0464 554 911. Closed Nov–Mar. There is another hostel in **Verona** – Ostello della Gioventù, salita Fontana del Ferro 15, tel: 045 590 360. Near the Teatro Romana. Take bus 73. Recommended evening meals.

Lake Garda and Verona at a Glance

Camp Sites

There are numerous camp sites around the lake and to the south. The following are recommended:

Rucc, via Rimenbranze 23, Gargnano, tel: 0365 71805.
Serenella, Riva, tel: 045 721 1333, fax: 045 721 1552.
La Rocca, Riva, tel: 045 721 1111, tel/fax: 045 721 1300.
Sirmione, via Sirmioncino 9, Sirmione, tel: 030 990 4665.
Verona, Campeggio Castel San Pietro, Via Castel San Pietro, Verona. Next to the youth hostel. Tel: 045 592 037. Note that nearly all camp sites in the Garda area are closed from November to March.

WHERE TO EAT

There are plenty of eating options around Lake Garda and in Verona. The classiest restaurants are often in the large hotels, but rarely serve Italian regional dishes. For these, try the local trattorias.

LUXURY

Vecchia Riva, via Bastione 3, Riva, tel: 0464 555 061. Outstanding Italian cuisine. Need to book. Closed Tue.
Vecchia Laguna, piazzale Vecchia Laguna 1, Sirmione, tel: 030 919 012. Known for its fish menu.
Al Caval, via Gardesana 186, Torri del Benaco, tel: 045 722 5666. Another restaurant famed for its lake fish.
Cavallino, via Gherla 30, Desenzano, tel: 030 912 0217.

Oustanding seafood, with lakeside terrace. Closed Mon.

MID-RANGE

La Terrazza, via Pasùbio 15, Torbole, tel: 0464 505 083. Good traditional food with lake views.
Accademia, via Scala 10, Verona, tel: 045 800 6072. Attentive service at this homely city centre restaurant.
Trattoria Bicocca, via Molini 6, Desenzano, tel: 030 914 3658. Atmospheric trattoria serving a variety of lake fish.
Trattoria al Combattante, San Bernardetto, Via Sabino, Peschiera, tel: 045 755 3227. Lake fish and antipasti are the specialities of this trattoria on the road to Sirmione.

BUDGET

Belvedere, via Serafini 2, Arco, near Riva, tel: 0464 516 144. Specializes in meat and home-grown vegetables.
La Terraza, via Roma 53, Gardone. Cheap and cheerful snacks and pizzas
Gondoliere, Piazza Matteotti, Malcésine. Very reasonably priced seafood.
Taverna Fregosa, corso Vittorio Emanuele II 37, Riva. Large helpings at this taverna on the old town's main street.

SHOPPING

There are plenty of opportunities for shopping in the street markets in the towns around Lake Garda. Bargains can be had in leather goods, metal-

work, carved wooden objects and ceramics. The area to the south and east of Lake Garda specializes in the production of wine and olive oil, and there are a number of outlets where these items can be bought directly from the producer. Verona is particularly good for high-quality shoes.

TOURS AND EXCURSIONS

Local tour operators offer excursions from the lake resorts to historic towns such as **Bergamo**, **Mantua** and **Verona**. The most popular venues by the lake itself are the Gardaland theme park near Peschiera and **Il Vittoriale** at Gardone. With a comprehensive network of passenger boats on the lake, it is easy to plan your own tours.

USEFUL CONTACTS

Tourist Information Offices:
Sirmione, tel: 030 916 114.
Gardone, via Repubblica 39, tel: 0365 20347.
Gargnano, Palazzo Communale, tel: 0365 71222.
Riva del Garda, Giardini di Porta Orientale, tel: 0464 554 444.
Torbole, tel: 0464 505 177.
Malcésine, via Capitanato 6–8, tel: 045 740 0044.
Torri del Benaco, tel: 045 722 5120.
Garda, via Don Gnocchi 23, tel: 045 627 0384.
Verona, Piazza Brà, tel: 045 806 8680, website: www.verona.it

Travel Tips

Tourist Information

The **Italian State Tourist Office** (ENIT) has offices abroad in USA (New York, Chicago and Los Angeles), Canada (Montreal and Toronto), Australia (Sydney) and the Republic of Ireland. The address of the UK office is: ENIT, 1 Princes Street, London, W1R 8AY, tel: 020 7408 1254, fax: 7493 6695. These offices are useful before departure, providing maps, brochures, transport details and lists of accommodation. Within Italy itself there are regional and provincial tourist boards. All cities, towns and airports will have a tourist office usually known as an **APT** (*Azienda per il Turismo*) and shown with the standard 'i' symbol. APT's are found in the following towns and cities:

Milan: via Marconi 1, (next to the cathedral), tel: 02 7252 4301, fax: 7252 5250. There is also an office at the Stazione Centrale, tel: 02 669 0432, website: www.vivamilano.it

Bergamo: viale Vittorio Emanuele II 20, tel: 035 213 185, fax: 230 184, website: www.bergamo.it

Brescia: corso Zanadelli 38, tel: 030 45052, fax: 293 284, website: www.bresciaholiday.com

Como: piazza Cavour 17, tel: 031 269 712, fax: 261 152, website: www.lakecomo.com

Cremona: Piazza del Comune (opposite the cathedral), tel: 0372 23233, website: www.cremonaturismo.com

Monza: Piazza Communale, tel: 039 323 222.

Pavia: via F. Filzi 2, tel: 0382 22156, fax: 32221.

Stresa: Via Principe Tomaso, tel: 0323 30150, fax: 32561, website: www.lagomaggiore.it

Varese: via Carrobio 2, tel: 0332 283 604.

Verona: Piazza Brà, tel: 045 806 8680, website: www.verona-apt.net

Entry Requirements

All visitors to Italy need a valid passport. Citizens of EU countries, including the UK and the Republic of Ireland, can stay as long as they like. Visitors from USA, Australia, Canada and New Zealand can stay for up to 3 months before requiring a visa. Visitors from other countries should consult their embassies regarding visas. It is a legal necessity to register with the police within three days of entering Italy – your hotel or camp site automatically do this for you. Anyone on holiday who decides to register with the local police station will probably be greeted with baffled amusement!

Customs

EU regulations apply, so that there is a free exchange of non-duty-free goods for personal use for citizens of these countries. There is little point in bringing in duty-paid goods as tobacco and alcohol are as cheap or cheaper here than in other European countries. Visitors from non-EU countries are subject to restrictions which vary from country to country. The age limit for importing alcohol and tobacco is 17. There is no limit on the amount of traveller's cheques that can be imported or exported.

Health Requirements

The standard of health care in northern Italy is generally on a par with the rest of Europe and travellers should encounter few problems. EU residents should take Form E111 with them so that they can obtain treatment on the same terms as residents. Australia also has a reciprocal health care agreement, but visitors from other countries should take out travel insurance that includes health benefits. For minor medical problems, go to the nearest *farmacia*, open during normal shopping hours. There is generally a duty pharmacy open at other times. In Milan there is a 24-hour *farmacia* at the Stazione Centrale.

Getting There

By air: Milan has two airports, Linate and Malpensa. **Linate** (info tel: freephone 1673 37337) is 8km (5 miles) east of the city centre. As it is near Milan, it is popular with business travellers, and two low-cost airlines, **Go** (www.go-fly.com) and **Buzz** (www.buzzaway.com) run daily flights from Stanstead to Linate. In the future Linate will only handle domestic flights. **Malpensa** (tel: freephone 7485 2200) is 50km (31 miles) northwest of Milan. Terminal One deals with international flights and Terminal Two handles charters. Both **British Airways** (info tel: 0345 222 111) and **Alitalia** (info tel: 020 760 2711) offer daily flights to and from London. Alitalia also has connections with Boston, Chicago, Los Angeles, Miami and New York. All main international car hire firms have offices at Malpensa, but many visitors prefer to use public transport to Milan. A high-speed railway line connects the airport to the city, with trains at 30 minute intervals. There are two efficient coach lines. The Malpensa Shuttle drops passengers off at the Stazione Centrale, and the Malpensa Express connects with both the Stazione Centrale and the more central Piazzale Cadorna. Both coach lines run at 20-minute intervals. Airline passengers visiting Lake Garda can also use the British Airways flights to **Verona**.

By road: The UK is linked with Europe by car ferry and the Channel Tunnel. Once on the mainland you can drive all the way to Milan on the motorway system, but tolls can be expensive, particularly in Switzerland. At Italian frontier crossings it is possible to buy booklets for fuel coupons and vouchers for motorway tolls. Italian motorways are called *autostradas* – all are toll roads. The *autostrada* system in northern Italy focuses on Milan, with motorways leading off to all the major lakes. Traffic congestion in Milan can be awful and motorists are advised to leave their cars in the ATM car parks on the outskirts. Sightseeing is easy using public transport: metro, buses, trams and trolleys. Motorists are advised to have comprehensive cover and an international green insurance card. In cases of breakdown, call tel: **116**. Milan can also be reached by **coach**. Eurolines run services from the UK and other European countries to Milan, Verona and Bergamo. For bookings and information in the UK, tel: 020 7730 8235.

ROAD SIGNS

Entrata • Entrance
Incrocio • Crossroads
Lavori in Corso •
Roadworks
Passaggio a Livello •
Level Crossing
Rallentare • Slow down
Senso vietato • No entry
Sosta vietata • No parking
Svolta • Bend

By train: the quickest rail route to Milan from the UK is by Eurostar to Paris, then take the overnight service to Milan. Drivers can load their cars on the overnight **motorail** service at Bologna or Paris, arriving in Milan the following morning. Most trains arrive at Milan's **Stazione Centrale** (tel: freephone 1478 88088), from where buses and metro go to the city centre. The station has a tourist office, banks, restaurants, a supermarket and a 24-hour pharmacy.

PUBLIC HOLIDAYS

On public holidays shops are closed and public transport services often much reduced.
1 January • New Year's Day
6 January • Epiphany
Easter Monday
25 April • Liberation Day
1 May • Labour Day
15 August • Assumption (*Ferragosta*)
1 November • All Saints Day (*Ognissanti*)
8 December • Immaculate Conception (*Immaccolata*)
25 December • Christmas Day (*Natale*)
26 December • St.Stephen's Day (*Santo Stefano*)

What to Pack

Strong walking shoes are advisable for the lake region. You'll need a sweater for the evenings (except Jul–Aug). Rainwear is likely to be needed in spring and autumn. Do not wear shorts and beachwear when visiting churches. There are opportunities to swim from many of the lake shores and in the pools of the larger hotels – so pack a costume. The Milanese are more formal in their dress than in other parts of Italy – it is the fashion capital of Europe and designer gear features strongly in leisure and casual wear.

Money Matters

ATMs are found everywhere and accept all major cards. **Credit or debit cards** can be used at hotels, restaurants, petrol stations and most shops. American Express **travellers' cheques** are widely accepted. **The euro** replaced the lira on 1 January 2002. It is issued in notes of 5, 10, 50, 100, 200 and 500 euros, and the coins come in denominations of 1, 2, 5, 10, 20 and 50 cents and 1 and 2 euros.

Accommodation

Hotels or *alberghi* are rated from 1–5 stars (depending on facilities, not service standards). *Pensioni* are more modest. Most hotels have different rates in summer and winter, and some resort hotels in the lake region close in winter. Check if breakfast is included – you can usually get a cheaper, better meal in a bar. Lists of hotels and pensions are posted in tourist offices, but they are not obliged to make bookings. The decent hotels in Milan are often fully booked during trade fairs. Most hotels are in the city centre near Stazione Centrale and the Piazza della Repubblica. To book, contact Milano Hotels Central Booking, Piazza Missori, tel: 02 805 4242. Waterside hotels in the lake region can be expensive. There are **youth Hostels** (*Ostelli per la gioventu*) in Bergamo, Como, Mantua, Menaggio, Riva del Garda and Verona. Milan's Piero Rotta hostel is at viale Salmoiraghi 2, tel: 02 3926 7095. Italy's Youth Hostel Association is the *Associazione Italiana Alberghi per la Gioventu* (or AIG),

Pallazzo della Civilta del Lavoro, Quadrato della Concordia, 00144 EUR Roma, tel: 06 591 3702. An international membership card is needed, which can often be bought at the hostel. Hostels are closed during the day and may have a curfew at night. They are renowned for noisy school parties, particularly around the Easter period. **Camping** is popular. The lakes have fine waterside sites, but they are crowded and noisy in August. Milan has two sites on the outskirts of the city. Unofficial camping is frowned on by the police, but tourist offices have lists of official sites. To obtain a camping carnet and details of all Italy's camp sites, contact *Centro Internazionale Prenotazioni Campeggio*, Casella Postale 23, 50041, Calenzano, Firenze, tel: 055 882 382.

Eating Out

Milan's restaurants serve food from China, India, Mexico and Japan, with ubiquitous North American fast food, but do try some **Milanese specialities**. A *ristorante* offers antipasto, pasta, main course and dessert. Cheaper *trattorias* are more likely to serve regional dishes. Specialist restaurants include *spaghetterias* and *pizzerias*. For snacks, try a *tavola calde* or *panini* bar. **Vegetarians** are catered for at most eateries. Restaurants usually open from 12:00–15:00 and from 19:30 onwards. Many close on one day a week, typically Sunday, though in the lake area it is more likely to be on Monday.

CONVERSION CHART		
FROM	**TO**	**MULTIPLY BY**
Millimetres	Inches	0.0394
Metres	Yards	1.0936
Metres	Feet	3.281
Kilometres	Miles	0.6214
Square kilometres	Square miles	0.386
Hectares	Acres	2.471
Litres	Pints	1.760
Kilograms	Pounds	2.205
Tonnes	Tons	0.984
To convert Celsius to Fahrenheit: x 9 ÷ 5 + 32		

Transport

Getting around poses few problems, apart from traffic congestion in central Milan.
Road: Milan has an efficient public transport system, which is fortunate as driving a car in the city is very difficult. Outside Milan, the *autostada* system allows you to reach all parts of the area more easily.
Car hire: Cars and camper vans (*autonoleggios*) can be hired at the main airports, where firms such as **Avis** (tel: 02 669 0280), **Hertz** (tel: 02 669 0061) and **Europcar** (tel: 02 8646 3454) have offices. It is cheaper to hire in advance in your own country. There is a minimum age limit of 21 and a credit card will be required.
Public transport: Milan's city transport system is operated by *Azienda Trasporti Municipali (ATM)*, with buses, trolley buses, trams and the metro.
Buses and **trams** are orange, and their stops are marked with yellow signs. They are frequent but often crowded. Buy tickets before boarding. The green *Tram Turistico* departs from Piazza Castello on a two-hour tour with multilingual taped descriptions. Bus tours, run by Autostradale, depart from the cathedral square and last for three hours. Both tours are highly recommended. The **Metro** has four lines. Line one is shown on maps in red, line two in green, line three in yellow and line four (the latest) in blue. Trains run from 06:00 to midnight. ATM tickets can be used for all types of transport, though they cannot be used twice on the metro. As

well as day tickets, weekly and monthly passes can be bought; 24- or 48-hour tourist tickets are good value. Tickets must be bought in advance (from automatic machines, tobacconists and newspaper kiosks).
Taxis: White in colour, taxis (expensive) cannot be hailed and must be boarded at the official taxi ranks scattered around the city. Make sure that the meter is switched on at the beginning of the ride. There will be surcharges for night-time journeys, luggage and trips to the airports.
Train: Italy's national railway, **FS** (*Ferrovie dello Stato*), is efficient and inexpensive. Routes link Milan with all the lakes. Tickets can be bought at the stations and at travel agents. A number of passes are available. For exploring northern Italy by train the 'Travel at Will' (*Biglietto Turistico Libera Circolazione*) ticket is useful. Other passes include Flexicard and the Kilometrico. Details can be obtained from the Stazione Centrale and travel agents.
Boat: All the larger lakes are served by watercraft such as steamers, hydrofoils, paddle steamers and motor boats. Some are timetabled ferries for foot passengers or vehicles, while others cruise the lakes on excursions. Contact local tourist offices about daily or weekly passes. Services are considerably curtailed in winter.
Cycles and motorbikes: Cycling is popular and bikes can be hired in all major towns. It is not recommended in Milan, despite the existence of cycle lanes, as motorists can be

USEFUL WORDS AND PHRASES
Yes/No • *Si/No*
Please • *Per favore*
Thank you • *Grazie*
You're welcome • *Prego*
Good morning • *Buongiorno*
Good evening • *Buona sera*
Good night • *Buena Notte*
Excuse me • *Mi scusi*
Do you speak English? • *Parla inglese?*
I don't understand • *Non capisco*
Speak slowly • *Parla lentamente*
What/Who/Where? • *Che?/Chi?/Dove?*
How?/When?/Why? • *Come?/Quando?/Perché?*
Good • *Buono*
Bad • *Male*
Fast • *Rapido*
Slow • *Lento*
Big • *Grande*
Small • *Piccolo*
Hot • *Caldo*
Cold • *Freddo*

ruthless. Cycling around the lakes or in the Alpine foothills can make a delightful holiday. Motorbikes, mopeds and scooters can also be hired. Helmets are compulsory and there are minimum age limits. *The Globetrotter Travel Map of Milan and the Italian Lakes* is highly recommended. Free guides provided by the tourist offices are good for general purposes. The Touring Club of Italy's *Lombardia* is good, as is their street plan of Milan.

Business Hours

Unlike in the south of Italy, the afternoon siesta is becoming more rare in the north. Most businesses in Milan work a 09:00–17:00 day. Shops close on Saturday afternoons and Sundays and some may take a lengthy lunch break. Most museums and galleries close on Mondays, but may stay open until 20:00 in summer. Chemists (*farmacias*) usually open 09:30–19:30 Monday–Saturday. A rota for late and Sunday opening is posted in all chemists' windows.

Tipping

A service charge and VAT are added to most restaurant and hotel bills; no tipping is needed unless service is outstanding. It is customary to tip porters, usherettes in cinemas, bellboys and attendants. A gratuity of 10 per cent is usual for taxi drivers and tour guides.

Time Difference

Italy uses Central European time, normally 1hr ahead of GMT, 7hr ahead of US Eastern Standard Time. From the last weekend of March to the end of September clocks are put one hour ahead.

Communications

Although the Italian **postal system** has a poor reputation, most post offices in Milan and the north of the country work efficiently. They open 08:30–13:50 Mon–Fri and 08:30–12:00 Sat. There are post offices at Stazione Centrale and at Milan's two airports. Stamps can be bought at tobacconists. Public **telephones** are run by Telecom *Italia* and there are plenty in Milan and around the lakes. Public phones take coins and cards (from tobacconists and newsstands). GSM mobile phones can be hired at the Euro Business Centre at Malpensa Airport. A Telecom Office at Stazione Centrale allows you to make international calls and send and receive faxes. Milan's area code is 02. When dialling abroad from Italy, use 0044 for the UK, 001 for the USA, 00353 for Ireland, 0061 for Australia. **Internet Cafés** are appearing widely in Milan and other cities in the north of Italy.

Electricity

The supply is 220 volts and plugs have two or three round pins. Visitors should bring their own travel plug adapter from home.

Weights and Measures

Italy uses the metric system.

Health Precautions

Water is safe to drink and public fountains are plentiful. Bottled water is available too. **Food** in restaurants is normally hygienically prepared, but shellfish can cause upset stomachs. Prevent **sunstroke** by using a hat and a high-factor sunscreen. **Mosquitoes** can be a problem in the summer, so take an insect repellent.

Personal Safety

Though the lake region sees little crime, Milan, like many cities, does have petty theft. A few sensible precautions reduce the risk considerably. Carry only minimal cash and keep valuables in the hotel safe. Beware of pickpockets on crowded trains, buses and in public places. Avoid poorly lit places at night. Lock your car and never leave valuables on view. If you are a victim, report to the local police station (*questura*). Larger stations have a tourist department and can issue a report for your insurance company. The police emergency number is **113**.

Etiquette

Wearing shorts or beachwear in **churches** is offensive. Do not disturb worshippers during a service, particularly with flash photography. Milan is very fashion conscious; smart dress and formality are considered important. **Smoking** is banned on public transport (but usually tolerated in restaurants). Reaction to **topless sunbathing** varies, but it is usually not acceptable at hotel pools or on lakeside beaches.

GOOD READING

Carluccio, Antonio *Carluccio's Complete Italian Food*, Quadrille.
da Vinci, Leonardo *Notebooks*, Oxford University Press.
David, Elizabeth *Italian Food*, Penguin.
Ginsborg, Paul *A History of Contemporary Italy*, Penguin.
Jepson, Tim *Wild Italy*. Aurum Press.
McCarthy, Patrick *The Crisis of the Italian State*, Palgrave.
Murray, Peter and Linda *Art of the Renaissance*, Thames & Hudson.
Peterson, Mountford & Hollom *Birds of Britain and Europe*, Collins.
Procacci, Guliano *History of the Italian People*, Penguin.

INDEX